North West Waterway Walks

Volume 1: South of the Mersey

Guy Lawson

Preface

Plenty has already been written about Britain's canals and rivers from the perspective of the historian, or the navigator, but there is little in print which looks at them from the towpath. This book, essentially a series of walks around the North West's waterways to the south of the River Mersey, is aimed at walkers, as well as those with an interest in the history of the region's canals.

Broadly speaking, the walks in this book are located between Wales and the Pennines, and between the River Mersey and the South Cheshire border.There are all manner of curiosities to be found along the region's towpaths - from stop planks to seal off the canal, to sluices and weirs to protect the water level. Where possible, I have tried to explain the function of the various canalside objects.

The canals and rivers of the North West have had a fairly chequered history, and none more so than those in the southern section of the River Mersey's catchment area. The industrial revolution led to the building of narrow canals, and to the region's rivers being made navigable. It may seem surprising today, but in the eighteenth century, there were protests about the building of canals similar to those made now about the construction of more motorways. Although canals were initially owned by private companies, they nevertheless did much to enhance the economy of the North West, by providing routes to the sea, and to Britain's major industrial towns and cities.

All that has changed, however, and little commercial traffic can be found on the region's waterways. For a good many years, they lay unused and forgotten. Over the last twenty five years, however, pleasure craft have taken over and, although enthusiasts may be nostalgic for the great days of the canal age, holiday makers both bring tourism to the area and keep the waterways open.

Many of the North West's waterways pass through delightful and unspoilt scenery - wooded cuttings that are hidden from the world, or high embankments that provide splendid views across towns and countryside. One of my favourite waterways, the River Weaver runs through some particularly attractive settings and yet still has some commercial traffic. There is something curiously impressive about the sight of an ocean-going freighter passing through the remote locks at Saltersford.

Now, with the existence of bodies like the National Rivers Authority and the Mersey Basin Campaign, strenuous efforts are being made to clean up the region's waterways - not to do away with the canals' industrial heritage altogether, but to make it more accessible and to present it in a more favourable light. It all takes time, however, and it will be some years before the job is completed. There are signs of improvement already, and the general increase in interest in the North West's waterways will, at least, help to ensure that work continues. It may seem surprising that, in the last century, the apprentices in Warrington complained at being presented so many times with salmon, caught from the River Mersey, for lunch, but salmon have again been sighted working their way up the river.

Without the work of enthusiasts, the waterway network would be in nothing like such good condition. It was largely through the work of volunteers that Marple Locks, and therefore the Cheshire Ring, were saved from the threat of closure and restored. Fortunately, towpaths in the North West are well-kept and in good condition, but some could do with improvement. Although I would have liked to include more walks alongside the River Weaver, for example, there are sections of the towpath where it has been swallowed up by woodland or by the river itself. Brave it by all means, but wellington boots are essential.

The North West is particularly lucky to have such a rich mixture of waterways, and ones with a great deal of history. For those with an interest in wildlife, there are many stretches where, among other species, herons and kingfishers can be seen at close range. The walks that follow are not restricted to the prettiest stretches, but fair warning is given about those which involve the more urban landscapes!

Guy Lawson

CONTENTS

Llangollen and Shropshire Union Canals

Trent and Mersey Canal, Runcorn and Latchford Canal, and the River Weaver

The Bridgewater Canal and The Manchester Ship Canal

Compstall Navigation, Peak Forest and Macclesfield Canals

Location Map (West Section)

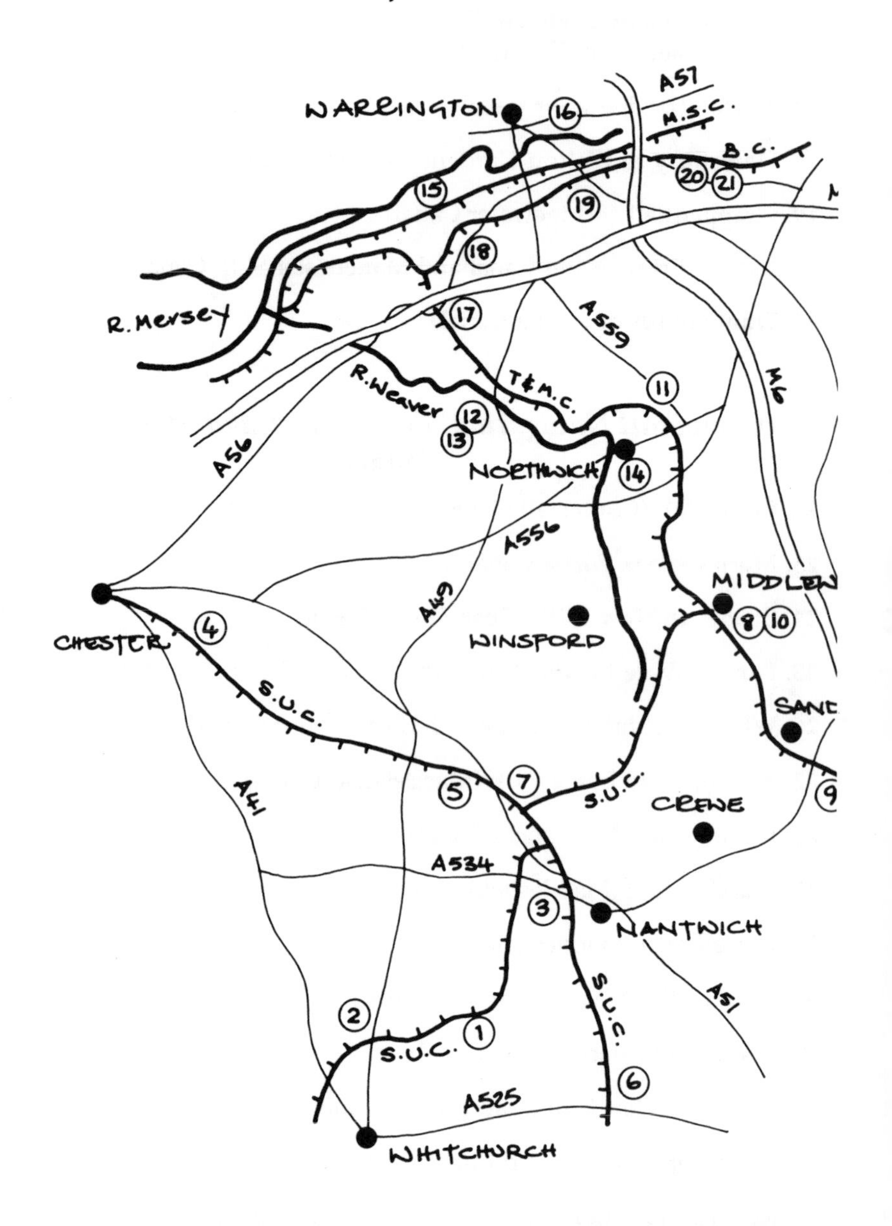

Location Map (East Section)

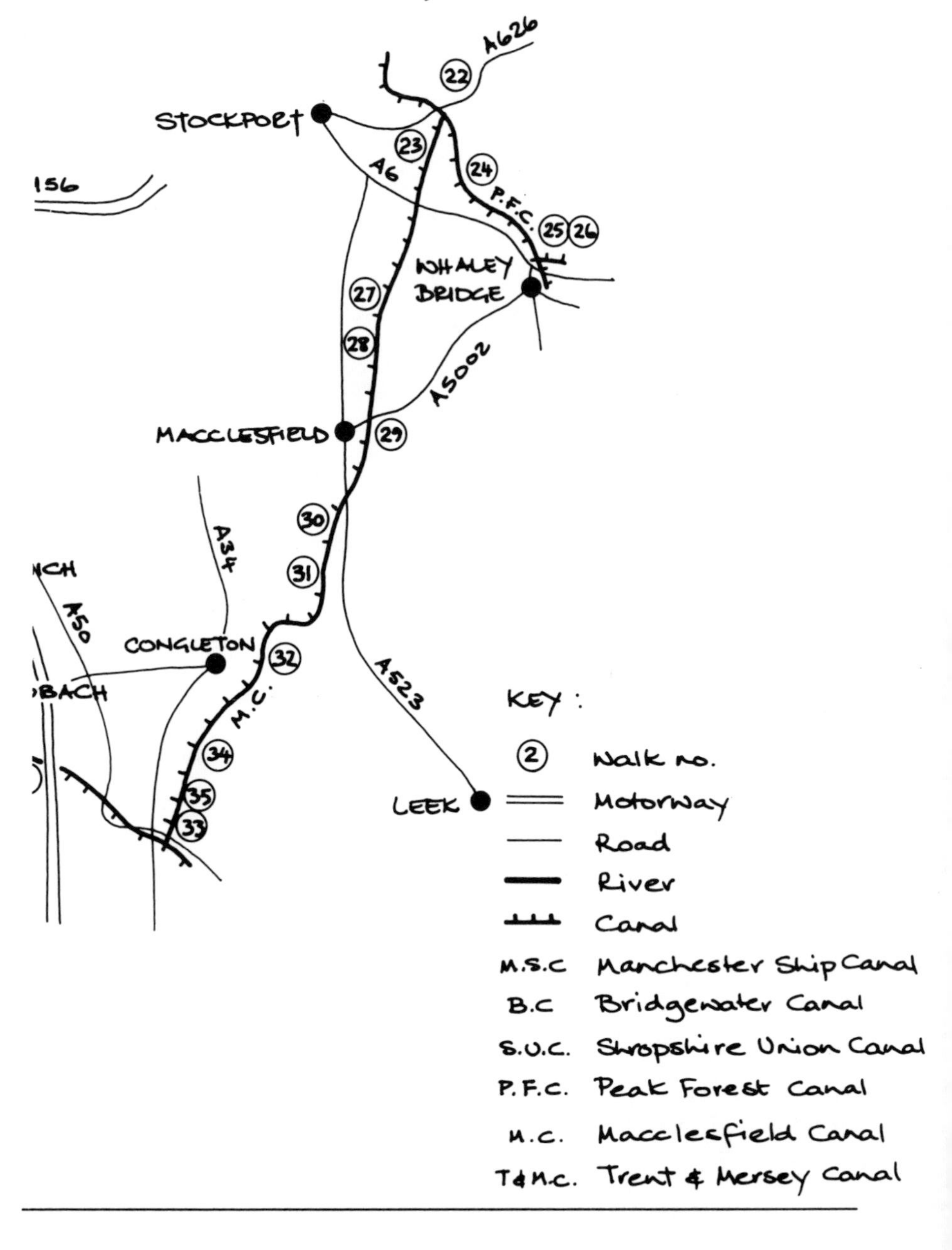

WALK 1: WRENBURY

Waterway: Llangollen Canal

Distance: 6 miles

Start: Wrenbury Bridge. Map reference: 590/481

Map: OS Pathfinder 807

How to get there: About five miles north of Whitchurch on the A49, turn right at Cholmondeley, and follow minor roads (which are fairly well signposted) for three and a half miles to Wrenbury. By bus from Whitchurch, take the 9A, or some C1 services.

This is a tricky walk. There are overgrown sections, and paths which do not appear to exist, so it should be navigated carefully. Although it is only about six miles, the walk takes in some fairly mixed terrain, so good footwear is essential. Ornithologists should find the walk particularly interesting as the many meres dotted along this stretch of the Llangollen canal are home to a great many species of waterfowl and wading birds.

To get to Wrenbury, take the minor road east off the A49 at Cholmondeley (about five miles north of Whitchurch). The village is signposted, and it is about three and a half miles to Wrenbury Bridge.

The Walk:

Start the walk from Wrenbury Bridge, and head west along the towpath.

Wrenbury Bridge is one of the unusual 'lift bridges' that are found on the Llangollen Canal. The canal is narrow and busy here and, in summer, boats often have difficulty in passing. Within a quarter of a mile from the bridge, there is a splendid view across the fields of Wrenbury Church with its squat sandstone tower and weather vane. On the left of the towpath, a stream runs parallel. This is the River Weaver in its early stages, not far from its source in the Peckforton Hills. It is not far to the next bridge (21) - another of the 'lift' type, which often remains raised, as it is only used by cattle.

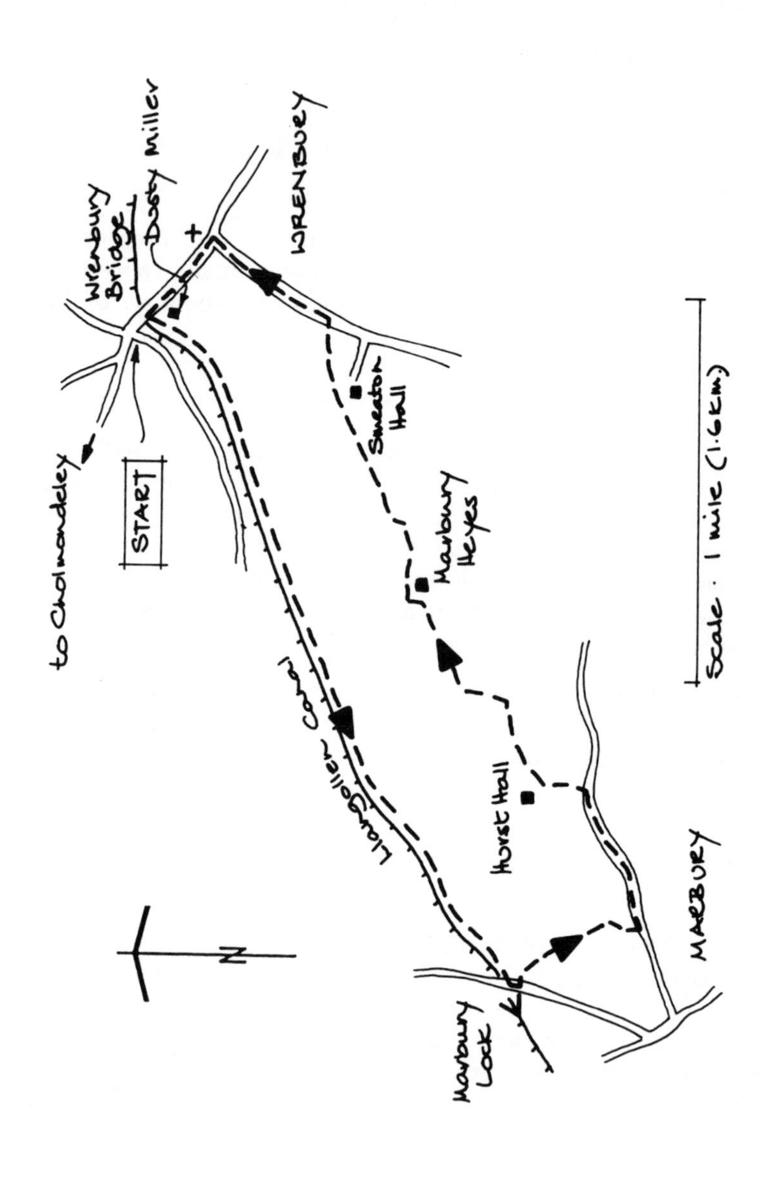
Wrenbury Bridge
Dusty Miller
WRENBURY
to Cholmondeley
START
Sweeton Hall
Marbury Heyes
Llangollen Canal
Hurst Hall
MARBURY
Marbury Lock
N
Scale · 1 mile (1.6Km)

Wrenbury Lift Bridge

In the distance, on the left hand side, the monument in the grounds of Combermere Abbey is visible. It is an obelisk, built in 1865 to commemorate Field Marshal Viscount Combermere. Combermere Abbey was founded by Cistercians in the 12th century, although little of the original building remains today. After the dissolution of the monasteries, the Cotton family took over the house. Just beyond bridge 21, there is a sluice gate beside the towpath, with winding gear, to drain excess water from the canal into streams that lead in to the Weaver. The towpath is thickly wooded with oak trees, and willows stand on the opposite bank. Just before the brick bridge 22, there is a row of pines - an unusual sight beside the region's canals.

After the bridge, the canal widens slightly, and is fed on the opposite bank by a stream, keeping the level high. The towpath is not well-used, and is rather overgrown in part. On a hill to the right, are the villages of Gaunton's Bank and Norbury. Beside the towpath, there is a wood, and a stream continues to run parallel

The canal bends gradually round, and Church Bridge (23) comes into view. Just before it is a roaring sluice channel on the opposite, pouring water down from the highter pound above the lock. Set a few feet behind church bridge is Marbury Lock, which raises the canal by six feet. It is a narrow, pretty lock, with a lock keeper's cottage.

Leave the towpath, and take the path up to the bridge, turn left, follow the road over an old stone bridge which was built over the streams that runs alongside the canal, and it is a short distance to a footpath sign on the left hand side. Cross over a rather rickety stile into a field. There is scarcely any trace of the path, so head diagonally across the field towards two gates that are set into the fence.

Take the right hand gate, and enter a field that rises quite sharply. There is still no sign of path, but the direction is marked by a row of substantial oak trees in the middle of the field. St Michael's church, Marbury then comes into view - another of Cheshire's sandstone-towered churches. (If the field is too overgrown, follow the edge, heading to the left at first, around to the opposite side.) Beyond the oak trees, and in line with them, there is a primitive stile on the far side of the field. Cross into the next field. Turn right, and follow the hawthorn hedge around it, as it works its way downhill. This leads to another stile in the bottom right hand corner of the field. Cross over, and follow the left hand edge of the next field to a gate about a hundred yards away where the footpath joins a road.

Once at the road turn left, and head up hill for about half a mile, and take the track off to Hurst Hall, the first farm on the left hand side. Follow the track for a few hundred yards, and there is a stile set in the fence on the right, before the gates of the farm. Cross over into a field, turn left, and follow the edge. At the far left hand corner, go through a gap in the fence and in the next field, follow the left hand edge as far as a telegraph pole, where there is a gap in the fence that leads downhill to the left. The path is not clearly marked, but is lined by two hedges. Keep following the left hand edge as it swings round to the right. This leads to another stile (with a yellow arrow on it).

Cross over onto a well-made track, and turn left. Follow it until it peters out, soon after crossing a small brook. Bear to the right towards a stile at the edge of the field. Over the stile, turn right, and follow the edge of the field to the next stile. Cross over, and follow the left hand edge of the next field, heading directly towards a farm. Just before the farm buildings, there is a stile leading off to the left. Cross over, and it is about 30 yards to a stile set into the right hand side of the next field. This leads to a set of steps, which cross a stream, and goes up to another stile on the other side. Once over this stile, turn left, and follow the edge of the field around, past rows of beech saplings. This leads to a stile with a yellow arrow on it. Cross over, turn right and follow the edge of the field. Fifty yards later, there is another stile.

Once over, bear slightly to the right, following the line of a large barn towards the far side of the field, where there is a stile made from wooden poles; this is followed by a narrow bridge, leading over a brook. On the other side of the brook, head in the general direction of the next farm. The last time I followed this path, there was a herd of deer in the field to the right. The path comes out by a yellow arrow and a gate leading on to a well-made track. Follow the yellow arrows to skirt the farmyard, and it is less than half a mile across a field to a road.

Although the path is not clear, yellow arrows clearly painted on trees mark the route. If the route becomes utterly unclear, ask the farmer if you can cross through his farmyard, and onto the drive leading onto the road, about a quarter of mile further back from where the path meets the road. Once on the road, turn left. The road crosses the River Weaver by a stone bridge - it is interesting to observe how narrow it is and how fast it flows. Close to Wrenbury village green is St Margaret's church, Wrenbury, which was paid for by the Cholmondeley family in the 15th century, although re-built in the 19th century.

Turn left, and it is only about a quarter of a mile downhill to the bridge across the canal, and the start of the walk. On the way down, The Cotton Arms is on the right, named after Sir John Stapleton Cotton. Sir John, who lived at Wrenbury Hall, set some way out of the village, was one of Wellington's Generals and became the first Lord Combermere. His statue is in Chester Cathedral. Refreshments can also be bought at the Dusty Miller, on the opposite side of the road, right by the canal.

WALK 2: MARBURY

Waterway: Llangollen Canal

Distance: 7 miles

Start: Quoisley Bridge on the A49. Map reference: 539/464

Map: OS Pathfinder 807

How to get there: Take the A49 north out of Whitchurch, and it is three miles to the bridge. By bus from Whitchurch, take the 9A Wrenbury service.

This walk is about seven miles long, and passes through some particulary unspoilt countryside. It is close to the point where Clwyd, Shropshire and Cheshire meet, and there are fine views of all three counties. Those with an interest in architecture will find a wealth of splendid buildings which have so far remained unaffected by the lure of tourism. Equally, ornithologists will be intrigued by the waterfowl sanctuary at Bradeley Green. Gourmets and gourmands alike will not be disappointed by the eating houses that the route passes. There are muddy stretches along the walk, so boots or strong shoes are recommended.

The Walk:

Start the walk from Quoisley Bridge. It is about three miles north of Whitchurch, where the A49 crosses the Llangollen canal. The towpath is on the north side of the bridge, and you follow it towards the lock which can be seen from the road. The canal runs parallel with the road as far as Quoisley Lock, which has a rise of six feet. After the lock, the canal and the road start to diverge. Land rises on both sides of the canal, and it is less than a mile to Willey Moor Lock. Beside the lock, the pub of the same name sells food and Greenall's beer.

Cross over Willey Moor Lock, and there is a clearly-marked track leading away from the lock towards the A49. Turn right on the main road for fifty yards, and on the opposite side is Bradeley Green

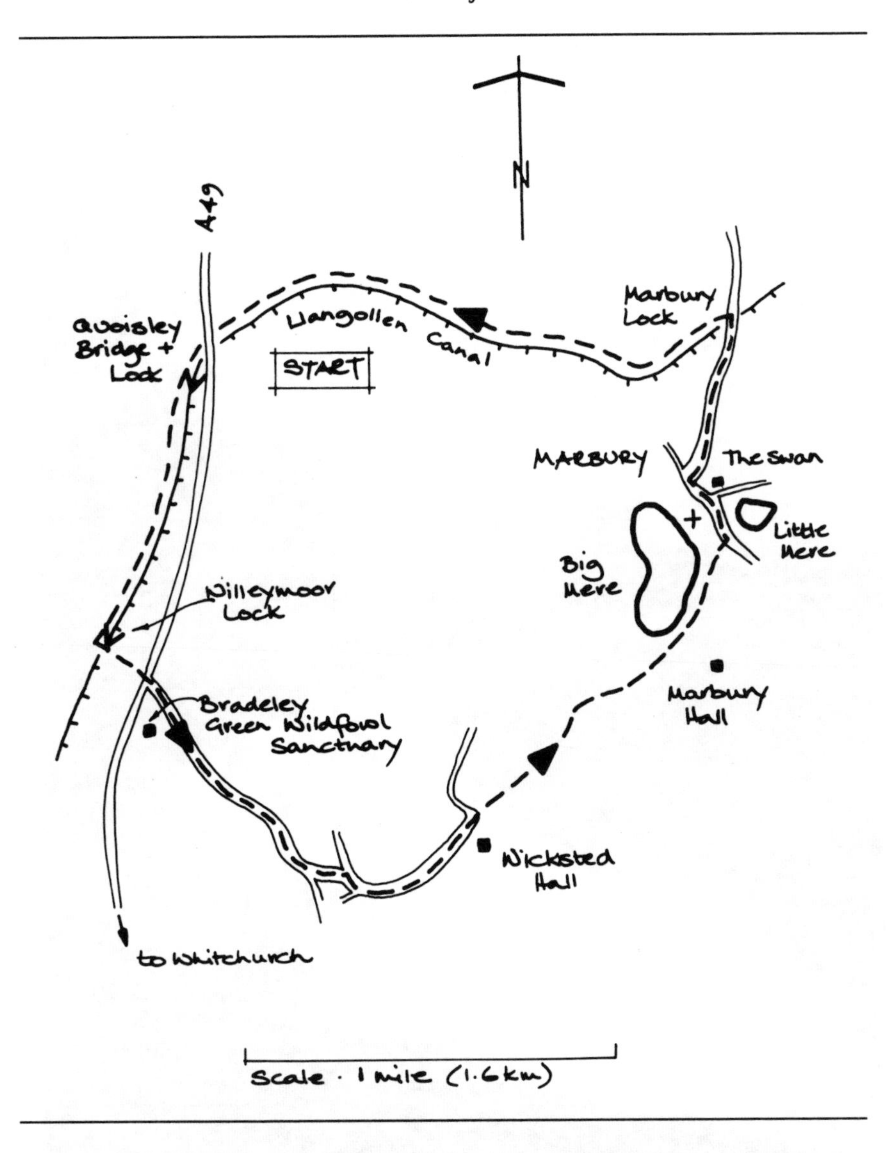

waterfowl sanctuary, with all manner of ducks and geese. Just before the sanctuary, follow a well-made track to your left. After less than half a mile, the track peters out, and divides into two. Do not take the right fork which leads towards a house, but follow the left, which rises

Llangollen Canal at Quoisley

The Swan Inn, Marbury

steadily uphill. This is often used as a bridle path, so it can get rather churned up by horses. A quarter of a mile from the junction, the path meets a wider track. Turn right, and follow it for half a mile until it meets a road.

Turn left, and follow the road. Past Wirswall Hall and Wicksted Farm on the right, it is only a few hundred yards to Wicksted Hall. Just beyond the drive to the hall, at a bend in the road, a path leads off to the right.

From the start of the path, there is a magnificent view of the Bickerton and Peckforton Hills. The path follows a beech hedge, to the right, gradually heading downhill and bearing gradually to the right. Do not follow the small path that heads off to the left. If in doubt, aim just to the right of the sandstone tower of St Michael's, Marbury. The church is perpendicular in style, with the usual 19th century alterations.

After about half a mile, the path runs alongside a wood which shields the 19th century Marbury Hall to the right. On the left, there is the larger of Marbury's two meres, and the path runs close alongside. The path comes out at a gate, onto a narrow road. Turn left, and it is about a quarter of a mile to the centre of Marbury. This is a spectacularly pretty village with its fifteenth century church, and 'The Swan', a particularly attractive inn which sells excellent food.

Take the road off to the left, leading to the church, and a couple of hundred yards later turn right. From here, it is about half a mile to Marbury Lock. Cross the bridge over the canal, and follow the towpath to the left. Marbury Lock seems very deep and narrow, and there is a lock keeper's cottage on the opposite side.

The canal is wooded and very peaceful along this stretch. It is also slightly raised, and a network of brooks and streams can be seen in the fields below. After a couple of sharp bends, the canal passes under Steer Bridge (24) and then runs along more open country for the next mile and a quarter, back to Quoisley Bridge (25) where the A49 crosses the canal.

WALK 3: ACTON TO HURLESTON JUNCTION

Waterways: Llangollen Canal, Shropshire Union Canal

Distance: 5 miles

Start: Acton church, on the A534 north of Nantwich. Map reference: 632/531

Map: OS Pathfinder 791

How to get there: The start is a couple of miles north of Nantwich on the A534 towards. By bus from Nantwich, take the C84 Chester service.

This is a gentle walk, about five miles long. It passes five locks, and one of the busiest canal junctions in the country. Parts of the walk can get rather muddy, but the towpaths are well kept, and unspoilt.

Start the walk from the village of Acton, a couple of miles outside Nantwich on the A534 towards Wrexham. It is hardly a village at all, more a strip of cottages along the main road, but it is very old. If you have time, the village is well worth exploring. Just before the church is The Star, an attractive old pub which sells Bass beers, and bar snacks. Worth noting is the mounting block set into the front wall.

In 1643, during the Civil War, the Parliamentarians, under Sir Thomas Fairfax routed the Royalists at Acton. A little way beyond the village on the right side, is Dorfold Hall, which still has part of its original moat. The hall is a fine example of Elizabethan architecture, and was completed in 1616 by Sir Ralph Wilbraham.The avenue of limes to the house was planted in the 19th century, and there is a fine set of iron gates.

Parts of St Mary's church date back to the 13th century. In 1797, the top of the tower collapsed, and was subsequently re-built. Rumour has it that, in the 19th century, a beadle used to walk up and down the aisle during services and tap on the head any of the congregation he saw falling asleep! At the front of the graveyard, there is a marble headstone by the grave of the cricketer, Albert Hornby, showing a set of stumps, a bat and a ball:

The Walk

Take the narrow road leading off to the right, just in front of the church. The footpath is on the right hand side of the road. Follow the road for about half a mile to a junction. Take the left turn into Swanley Road, for about a hundred yards, to where it comes to a crossroads. Take the left turn into the very narrow Ravens Lane. From the crossroads, there is a

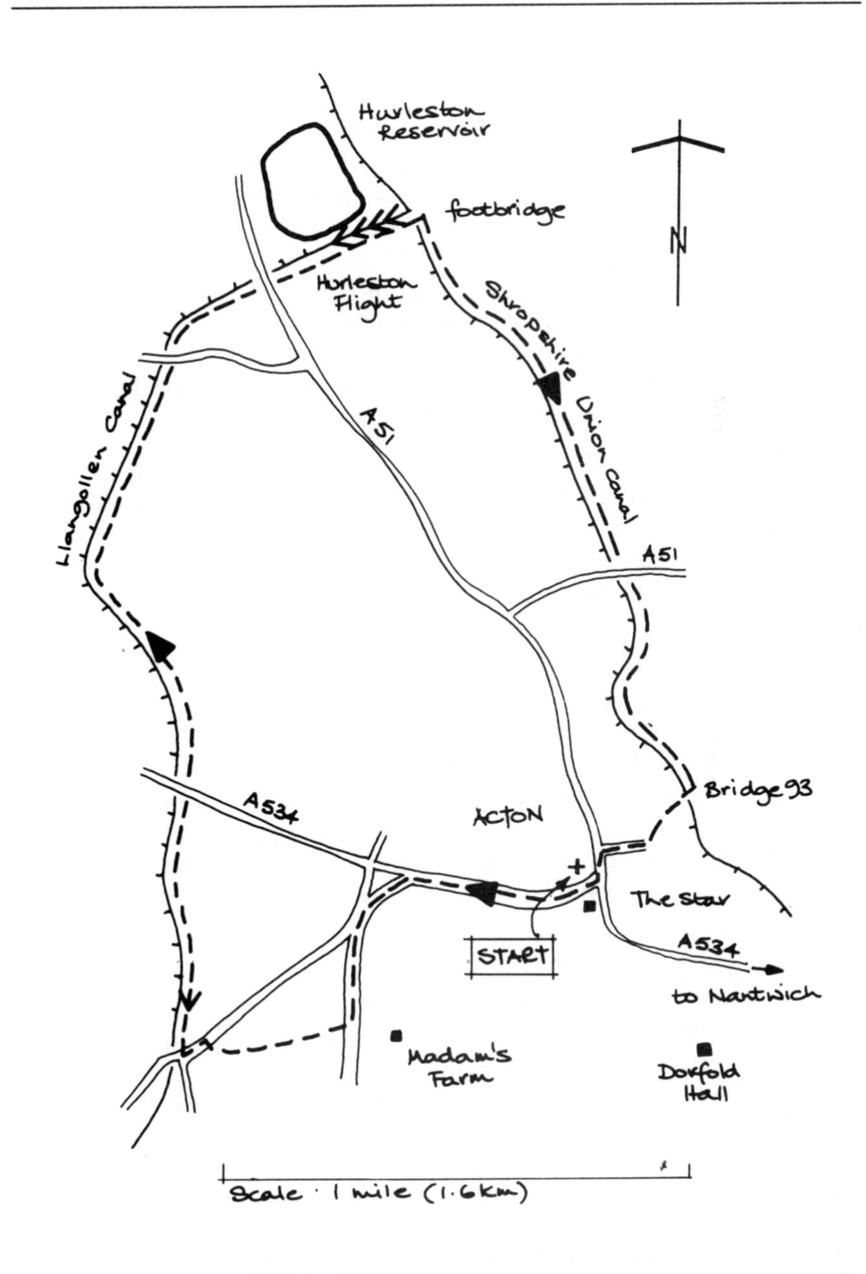
Hurleston Reservoir
footbridge
N
Hurleston Flight
Shropshire Union Canal
A51
Llangollen Canal
A51
Bridge 93
A534
ACTON
The Star
START
A534
to Nantwich
Madam's Farm
Dorfold Hall
Scale · 1 mile (1·6km)

very good view to the right of an old windmill - no sails now, but the rest is surprisingly well-preserved.

Less than a quarter of a mile down Ravens Lane is Madam's Farm. By the entrance, there are footpath signs on both sides of the road. The farm is an impressive three storey building. Follow the sign to the right, in the opposite direction ot the farm. Once in the field, it is immediately apparent that there is no path as such. If the field is muddy and ploughed up, follow the edge of the field to the right, working round to a gap in the edge on the opposite side to the road. There is actually a right of way across the field, so if it possible head straight across to the wide gap. This leads into another field. This time, follow the edge of the field to the right, past a wood of deciduous and evergreen trees, to a gap in the far right hand corner, beside a white post.

This leads into a lane. Turn right, and follow it for a hundred yards to where it joins a road. Turn left, and it is less than a quarter of a mile to a bend in the road, where it crosses the Llangollen Canal. On the left side of the bridge, there is a small pond with waterfowl on it. Take the steps down to the towpath on the right hand side, and head towards the lock.

Swanley No 2 Lock drops the canal by 6ft 3ins, with a fast flowing channel to its left, as is common on the Llangollen Canal. It is about half a mile from here to where the A534 crosses the canal at Burland. From here, the canal winds through agricultural land, for the most part given over to dairy farming. In summer, do not be too surprised to find cows in the water, as the canal is shallow near the edges, and some of the banks have become eroded. This stretch is often fairly busy with canal boats, being so close to the junction with the main line of the Shropshire Union Canal.

After the canal passes under the Nantwich to Chester Road, it comes to Hurleston Locks. There are four altogether, dropping the canal some 34ft 3ins in total, to its junction with the Shropshire Union. Above the first lock, there is a weir on the left hand side leading in to Hurlestone Reservoir, which has a capacity of 85 million gallons. The reservoir is unusual since, unlike other canal reservoirs, it is not fed by local streams, but relies on water being passed down the length of the Llangollen Canal, and fed in to it over the weir. In 1955, the Mid Cheshire Water Board formed an agreement, by which they could take water from the reservoir, and treat it for domestic consumption.

Beyond the locks is the junction. In summer, this is usually full of craft waiting their turn to enter the Llangollen Canal. Cross the footbridge beyond the locks to join the Shropshire Union Canal towpath, and turn right.

For part of the way, the canal is raised above the very low-lying land. The square tower of Acton Church is clearly visible along this stretch. Pass under Corne's Bridge (96), and then under the A51 road bridge. After this point, the canal winds through some tight bends. Running north from Nantwich to Chester, this stretch used to be called the Chester Canal, before the Shropshire Union was formed, and can be easily distinguished from the cuttings and embankments to the south of Nantwich by the fact that its route follows the windings of a contour line, and that it is a good deal wider.

At Acton Bridge (93), leave the towpath, cross over the canal bridge, and head towards a solitary oak dead ahead in the middle of a field. Beyond the oak, aim for a stile in the far side of the field. Cross over, and the path winds uphill, bearing left, alongside a bungalow. The path comes out into a small housing estate. Turn right where it meets the road, and it is a little over a hundred yards to the main road. Turn left, and it is two hundred yards to Acton Church, and the start of the walk.

WALK 4: WAVERTON AND TATTENHALL

Waterway: Shropshire Union Canal

Distance: Just over 8 miles

Start: Egg Bridge, Waverton. Map reference: 455/642

Map: OS Pathfinder 774

How to get there: From Chester, head south on the A41(T) towards Whitchurch, and turn left to Waverton. By bus from Chester, take the 12 Tarporley service.

In many ways, this at first seems one of the least prepossessing walks. There are no locks, the countryside is flat and relatively featureless, and there is little of historical interest along this stretch of the canal. Perhaps for these very reasons, some of the most curious architecture in North Cheshire has remained undiscovered. This walk is principally for those with an interest in curiosities: the church at Waverton, the bell tower at Hargrave, and the moated Huxley Lower Hall are all remarkable - and remarkably little known.

Start the walk from Egg Bridge (119), Waverton. Heading south from Chester towards Whitchurch on the A41(T), Waverton is about three miles along. Turn left into Egg Bridge Lane, and follow it to where it crosses the Shropshire Union Canal.

Waverton is a small village with a good selection of shops. Its main claim to fame, however, is its unusual church. St Peter's, Waverton has a pyramidal top, added in the late 19th century, to its Perpendicular tower. There are few points on this walk where refreshments may be bought, so Waverton is a useful place to stock up.

The Walk:

Join the towpath on the nearside of the bridge, and head to the right. The Shropshire Union Canal is wide along this stretch, and runs

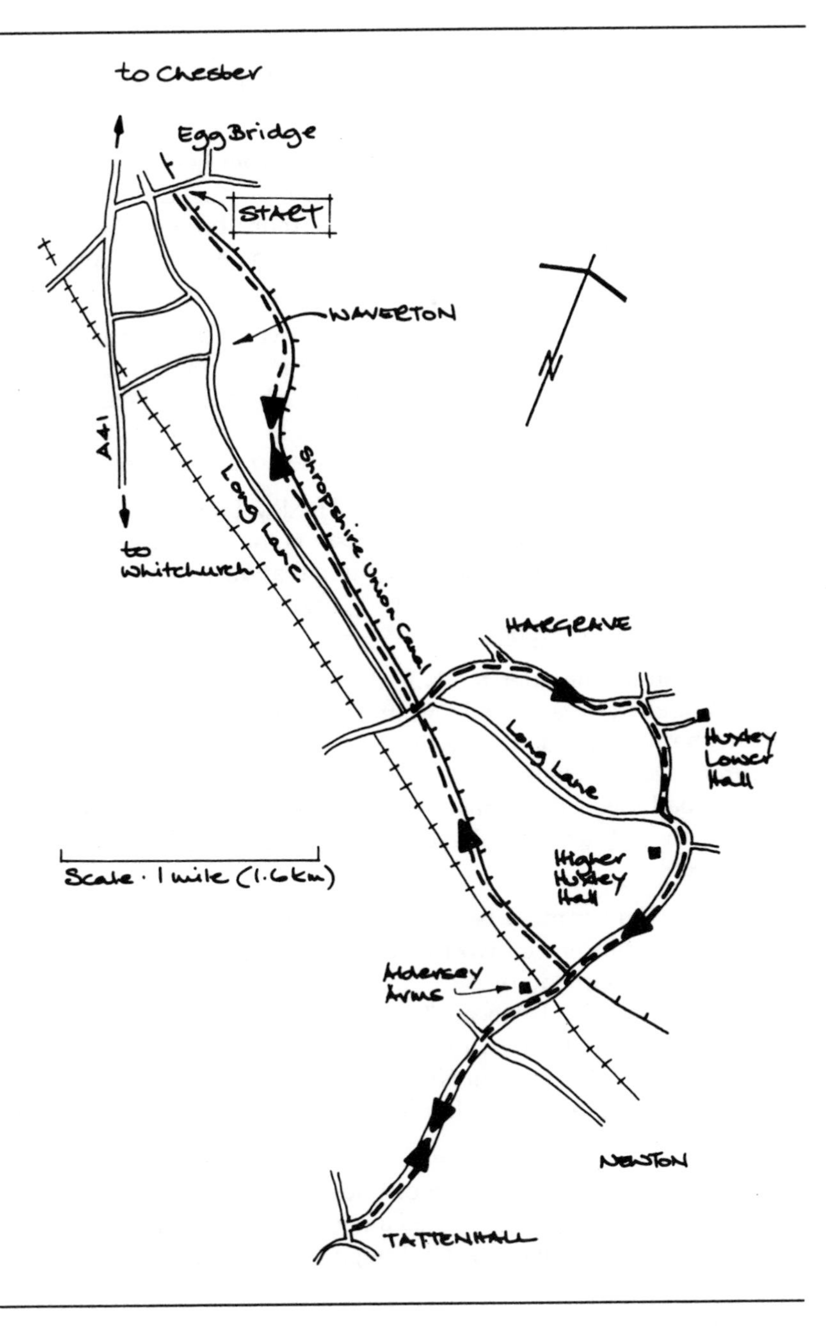
to Chester
Egg Bridge
START
WAVERTON
A41
to Whitchurch
Long Lane
Shropshire Union Canal
HARGRAVE
Long Lane
Huxley Lower Hall
Higher Huxley Hall
Scale · 1 mile (1.6km)
Aldersey Arms
NEWTON
TATTENHALL

through the flat expanses of the Cheshire plain. On the opposite bank is a boatyard, with its own slipway and dry dock. To the left, there are good views of the Welsh hills.

Follow the canal under Davies Bridge (118). From here, the canal winds gradually to the right, until it runs close by the Chester to Crewe railway line on the right. There are two more bridges: Salmon's and Faulkner's, then the canal follows a straight line as far as Golden Nook Bridge (115).

Take the path up to the bridge, and cross over. On the other side, the road forks. Follow the left fork into Hargrave. In the centre of the village, there is the attractive 17th century church, St Peter's, with its bell tower added in the last century. There is also an inscription to Sir Thomas Moulson, who subsequently became Lord Mayor of London.

Follow the road out of the village, and Huxley Lower Hall can be seen on the left hand side. All that is left today is the central section of what was once a much larger house, but its situation makes it particularly interesting. It is beside the River Gowy, and is ringed by a moat, which is crossed by a Jacobean bridge.

Less than half a mile after the hall, the road comes out at a T junction. Turn left, and the road winds around the more recent Huxley Higher Hall. At the next junction, take the road to the right, and follow it past the entrance to the Higher Hall on the right hand side. Less than a mile later, the road meets the canal at Crow's Nest Bridge (113). Just over the bridge is the attractive Aldersey Arms, which sells good food and Banks's beers.

Not far (less than a mile) beyond the Aldersey Arms is the village of Tattenhall, and this is well worth a detour. The village is most attractive with its timber framed cottages, and the church of St Alban. Equally worth a look are the Jacobean Tattenhall Hall, and Rose Corner. The latter, designed in 1927 by Clough Williams Ellis (the man responsible for the curious Portmeirion in North Wales), is notable for its grandiose facade which, despite its peculiarities, does not look out of place in the village.

Back to the walk. On the far side of bridge 113, rejoin the towpath, and head to the right. Almost immediately, the canal passes through a wooded cutting, but after Nixon's Bridge (114), it soon heads into open countryside again. It is just under a mile from here to Golden Nook Bridge, and the route back along the towpath to Waverton and the start of the walk.

WALK 5: BUNBURY TO BEESTON

Waterway: Shropshire Union Canal

Distance: Just over 7 miles

Start: Bunbury Locks. Map reference: 578/591

Map: OS Pathfinder 790

How to get there: From Tarporley, head south on the A51 towards Nantwich, the right turn to Bunbury is well signposted after about three miles. By bus from Nantwich, take the K56 Bunbury service.

Bunbury is a few miles south of Tarporley. Follow the A51 Chester to Nantwich road as far south as Alpraham, where the road to Bunbury is signposted to the right. After half a mile, the road crosses the Chester to Crewe railway line, then the Shropshire Union Canal. Just over the bridge, there is a path down to the towpath. This is a particularly interesting point to start the walk, being beside Bunbury's staircase locks. These large locks drop the canal 15 feet, and have to be navigated with care. There are two locks in the staircase, that is to say, the two locks are not separated by a pound, but empty from one to the other, and it is important to ensure that the bottom one is empty before running the top one into it.

Bunbury has always played an important role in the history of the Shropshire Union. The stables alongside the locks were once where the horses that pulled the boats were changed. Now they have been converted into boat-building workshops. Heading north on the canal, these are the first broad locks, with double gates at both ends, unlike the narrow locks south of Nantwich. Although the village itself is just over a mile from the canal, its square-towered church is worth seeing, and 'The Dysart Arms' sells food.

The Walk:

Follow the towpath down from the locks under bridge 105, past the marina. After a few hundred yards, the canal passes under the railway

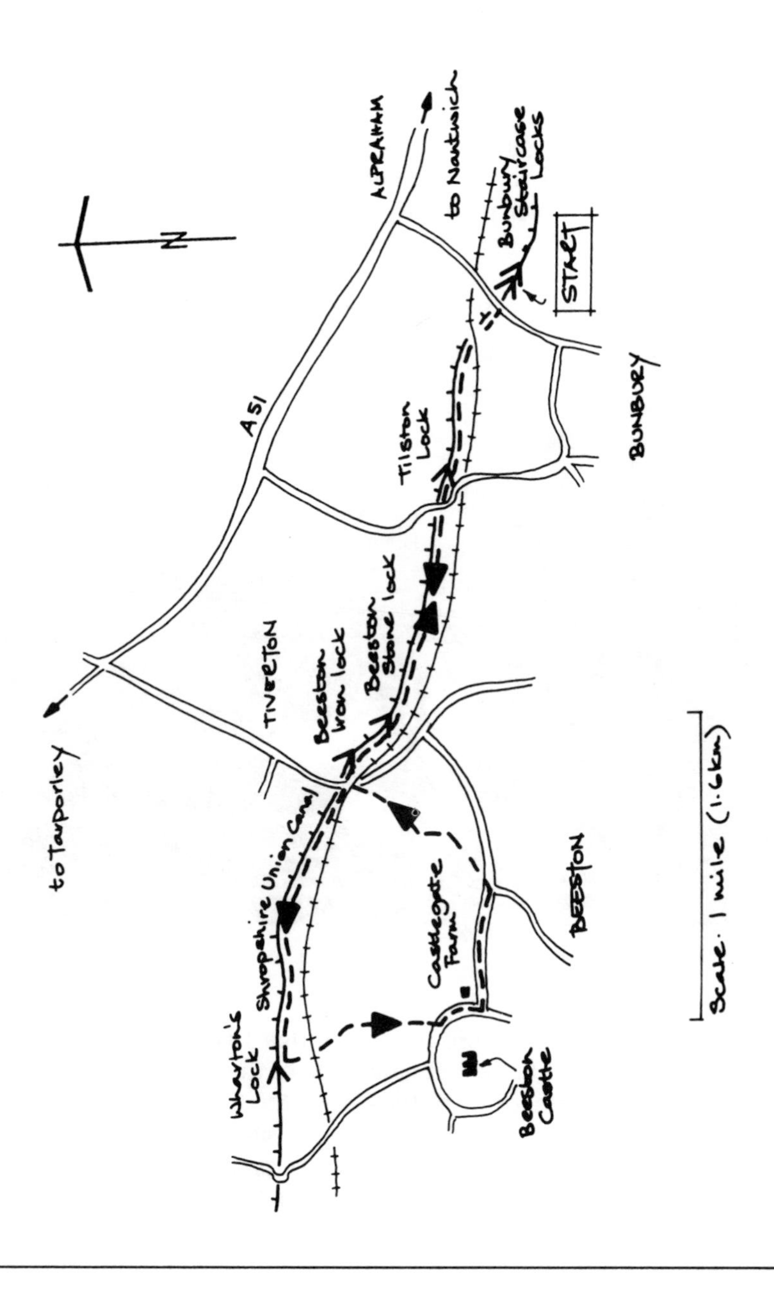
N
ALPRAHAM
to Nantwich
Bunbury Staircase Locks
START
BUNBURY
A51
Tilston Lock
TIVERTON
Beeston Iron lock
Beeston Stone lock
to Tarporley
Shropshire Union Canal
Castlegate Farm
BEESTON
Wharton's Lock
Beeston Castle
Scale: 1 mile (1.6km)

line, and into very pretty countryside. It is about a mile from here to Tilstone Lock - easily the prettiest of the broad locks with its pepperpot hut on the left hand side, dating from the days of the Chester Canal Company and its shady trees. From here, there is a superb view of Beeston Castle, dead ahead. When Bunbury Locks are busy, the great volume of water they contain sometimes proves too much for Tilstone Lock's sluices, and water pours over the lock's bottom gates. Follow the path under bridge 106, and a small brook emerges in the left hand side. This is the River Gowy, which rises in the Peckforton Hills, and comes out into the south side of the River Mersey near Ellesmere Port.

Tilstone Lock

The towpath is very well-kept beyond bridge 106, passing cottages with spectacular gardens. On the left hand side of the towpath, there is a line of willows. On the other side of the Gowy, the Chester to Crewe railway runs close by. To the right, the canal's opposite bank is lined with thick reed beds. It is surprising to find such a broad canal with so many bends in it. During the very hot summer of 1975, I took a narrow boat along this stretch, and the water level was so low that on one of these bends, the boat ran aground where the canal had silted up. The only way to get going again was to jump over the side and push - this is not recommended!

The canal gradually comes out into more open country, with a gorse-covered mound to the right. After another bend, the canal follows a straight course to Beeston Stone Lock. There is another pepperpot hut on the left side, and the cottage on the right sells home made jams and chutneys, as well as cakes, ice creams and snacks. It is not far from here to Beeston Iron Lock. It was built of iron plates bolted together, since earlier stone locks continually had problems with subsidence as a result of quicksand at the bottom of the lock. At the far end of the lock, one of the iron plates is dated 1828, and one can see how they have gradually bent out of shape over the years.

Immediately after the lock, the path goes under the A49, (bridge 107). On the other side, there is a little shop specialising in 'canalia'. The canal follows a straight contour line, and to the left, beyond the railway, are the buildings of Beeston Castle Market. A quarter of mile after the bridge, the wooded slopes on the opposite band come down to the canal, which then turns a wide bend. In the distance, straight ahead, there is a clear view of the Welsh hills. After half a mile, the canal comes up to Wharton Lock. Beyond the lock is an iron footbridge.

Cross over, and take the path, over a stile, up to the stone-arched bridge (108). Turn left, and go over the bridge. From the top, looking to the right, one can see the mossy cobbles of the sluiced channel coming out into the right hand bank. There is a stile on the other side of the bridge; cross over, and follow the path straight ahead, and aim for the bridge under the railway (it has an arrow painted on it). A little bridge crosses the Gowy, and the path leads down to the railway. There is a stile on either side of the arch beneath the railway.

On the other side of the railway, follow the path slightly uphill to another stile. The path runs through a field, and comes out at a well-made track, which bends left towards Castlegate Farm. Follow it up to the stile on the right hand side that leads onto the road. Beeston Castle is straight ahead with its thickly-wooded slopes rising steeply from the stone wall beside the road. Turn left, onto the road, and follow it along the castle's perimeter wall. Pass the farm, cross the road leading off left, and two hundred yards later, there is the entrance to Beeston Castle.

The way up to the castle starts through a stone gatehouse. There is a small admission charge. Beyond the gatehouse, there is a steep, but well-made path leading to the remains of the castle at the top. The castle is about 500 feet above sea level, with splendid views in all directions - the Welsh mountains to the west, the Pennines to the east, and the Wrekin to the south east. The castle itself dates back to the 13th century, but was virtually in ruins by the 16th century. It was in use again, however, during the Civil War. It has been suggested that, prior to that, there was an iron-age hill fort, and that the Romans made use of the natural vantage point. Legend has it that King Richard the Lionheart hid treasure in a deep well at the castle. Until gold or jewels are found, it will have to remain a legend.

From the castle gatehouse, turn left (facing away from the castle), and head back towards Castlegate Farm. Take the narrow road running downhill to the right. After less than half a mile, it joins a wider road. Turn left, and a few yards after the junction, a path leads off to the left. Take the path and, after a quarter of a mile, it joins a well made track heading towards Beeston Hall Farm. Turn left along the track and, after a couple of hundred yards, a path leads off to the right. Take this path which winds its way down to Beeston Market, and onto the A49.

At the road, turn left, go under the railway, and it is a very short distance to the canal. The towpath is on the nearside. Turn right, and follow it towards Beeston Iron Lock, and back along the Shropshire Union Canal to Bunbury Locks.

WALK 6: AUDLEM TO NANTWICH

Waterway: Shropshire Union Canal

Distance: 6 miles each way

Start: The Bridge Inn, Audlem. Map reference: 658/436.

Map: OS Pathfinder 808

How to get there: Follow the A529 south of Nantwich, then take the A525 towards Whitchurch. By bus from Nantwich, take the K61 or K63 services to Audlem.

This is a linear walk along one of the most rural and unspoilt stretches of any canal in the region. Right at the southern tip of Cheshire, the route passes through dairy farmland which produces the different varieties of Cheshire cheese. To Nantwich and back, the walk is about 11 miles. It is possible to catch a bus back, from Nantwich to Audlem, but check on the times that they run first. The towpath is in good condition and, although long, this walk is not strenuous.

Start the walk at Audlem, where the A525 Audlem to Whitchurch road crosses the Shropshire Union Canal. Audlem is about five miles south of Nantwich on the A529 towards Market Drayton. If approaching the walk from this direction, turn right at Audlem church, and head out of the centre of the village to the canal.

Audlem is very pretty. St James's church dates back to the 13th century. At the centre of the village is the 18th century buttermarket, and the attractive Lamb Hotel, which serves meals.

The Walk:

At the start of the walk is a charming pub, The Bridge Inn, which sells bar snacks and Marston's beers. Turn right, down the side of the pub, and follow the slope down to the towpath. This stretch always seems busy. Coming in the middle of a flight of fifteen locks, which raise the canal by 93ft, this is a good place for navigators to stop for a breather.

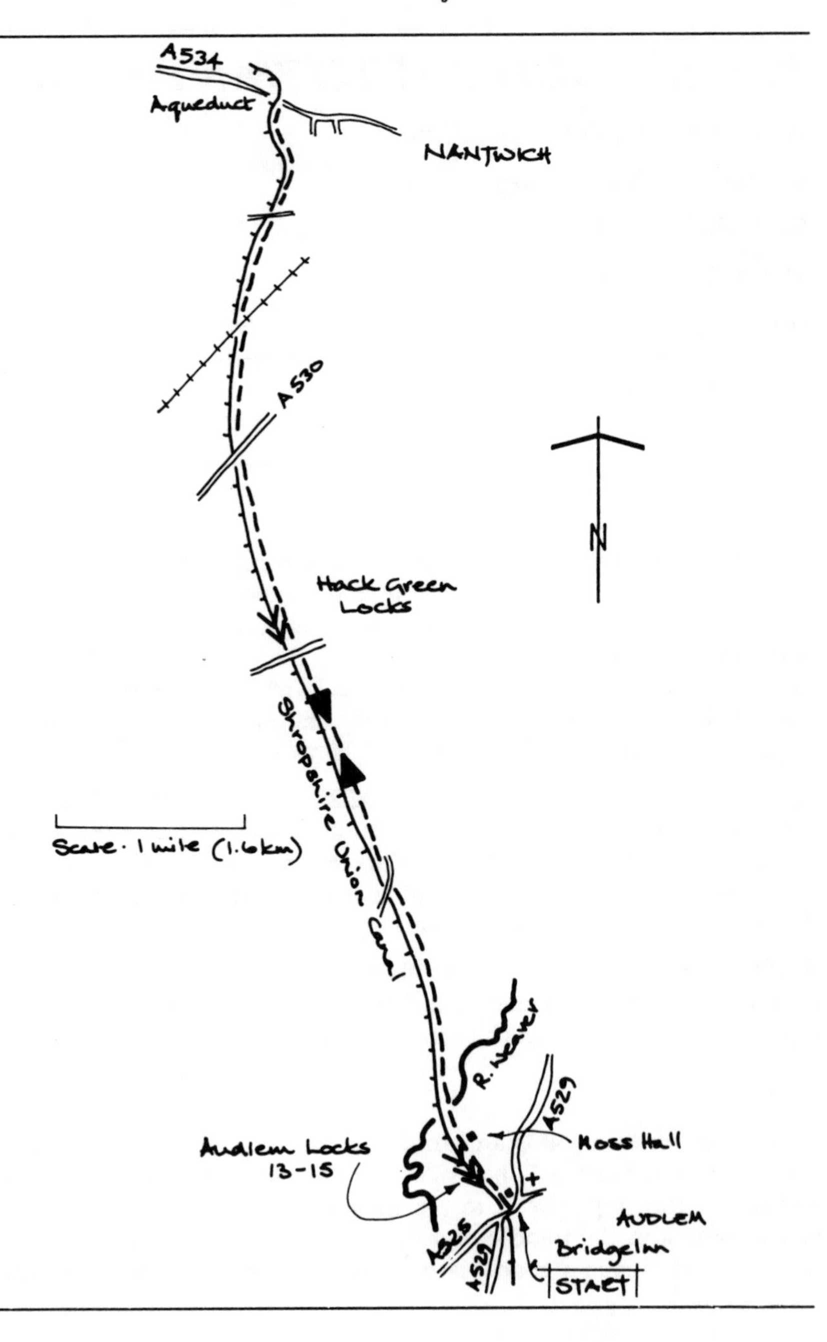
A534
Aqueduct
NANTWICH
A530
Hack Green
Locks
Shropshire Union Canal
Scale · 1 mile (1.6km)
R. Weaver
A529
Moss Hall
Audlem Locks
13-15
AUDLEM
A525
A529
Bridge Inn
START
N

In the opposite direction, there are twelve locks raising the canal up to the Shropshire border. Straight ahead, are the remaining three in the flight.

Before arriving at lock 13, Audlem Mill is to the right of the towpath, selling attractive canal souvenirs. Just beyond is another pub, The Shroppie Fly, which has part of a narrowboat forming its bar. Follow the path downhill past the lock, and the canal soon enters open countryside. Locks 14 and 15 are close together, separated by a short pound - the stretch of water between locks. Just after the last of the flight, there is a bridge (79) leading to Moss Hall, on the right hand side of the canal, which is a timber-framed house built in 1616.

Beyond the bridge, the canal is raised above the low-lying pastures by an embankment. The small river at the foot of it is the River Weaver in its early stages. It is hard to imagine that, in the 1940s, there were plans to make the Weaver navigable as far as the Shropshire Union Canal, and join it by means of a vertical lift, similar to the one at Anderton. By replacing the locks between Audlem and the end of the Shropshire Union near Wolverhampton with similar lifts, it was envisaged that trade could be developed on high capacity barges between the Mersey and the Midlands.

Following the straightest route possible, the canal runs along a fairly high level, providing good views across South Cheshire's farming land. After Coole Lane Bridge (82), the canal passes the remains of an old railway line between Nantwich and Market Drayton. It is just over a mile from here to Hack Green. Just beyond Burrow's Bridge (85) are Hack Green Locks. By the top lock are the old stables, dating back to horse-drawn narrowboats, which are now used for storage by the British Waterways Board.

Soon after the bottom lock, the canal runs alongside wooded countryside, and then across a short embankment. Navigating the Shropshire Union's embankments can be far from easy, as the wind can force boats off course, or into the bank. After Baddington Bridge (86), the canal runs through a cutting, before crossing one of the many streams feeding the Weaver, and then passing under the Shrewsbury to Crewe railway line.

Beyond the next two bridges, David's (90) and Marsh Lane (91), the canal runs into the outskirts of Nantwich. Follow the towpath along the steep embankment, built by Thomas Telford with its elegant ironwork. On the far side, a set of steps lead down to road. Head away from the bridge, and the centre of Nantwich is about half a mile. To return to the start of the walk, follow the towpath back.

Nantwich Basin

WALK 7: BARBRIDGE TO NANTWICH

Waterway: Shropshire Union Canal

Distance: 3 miles each way, or 6 miles if the circular route is taken.

Start: Barbridge Junction beside the A51. Map reference: 613/570

Map: OS Pathfinder 791

How to get there: Barbridge is about four miles north of Nantwich, on the A51. By bus from Nantwich, take the C84 Chester service.

This is a linear walk, with an optional circular route. Following the towpath in both directions, however, reveals the change in character of the Shropshire Union Canal, from a narrow canal to a wide canal. There and back, it is 6 miles, along well-kept towpaths. Detours, which are highly recommended, to Acton and to the centre of Nantwich, make the walk about 10 miles long. There are plenty of places to buy refreshments.

The Walk:

Start the walk from Barbridge Junction on the Shropshire Union Canal. Barbridge is about four miles out of Nantwich along the A51 towards Chester. It is the junction of the main line of the Shropshire Union Canal, and the Middlewich branch, which used to be known as the Wardle Canal. On the left hand side of the road is the Jolly Tar, a modern pub selling Greenall's beers. Take the next right after the pub, and this leads up to bridge 101. Cross over, and follow the track to the right. This leads to the bridge across the entrance to the Middlewich branch.

The track becomes the towpath. Just south of the junction, the canal narrows, and this is where a covered warehouse was built right across the canal. This is a busy stretch, with many permanent moorings, being at something of a crossroads between the Middlewich Branch, the

Llangollen Canal (which joins a mile to the south), and the Shropshire Union. On the opposite side of the canal is the Barbridge Inn, which serves good food and Boddington's beers.

Barbridge Junction

The canal passes under Bremilow's Bridge (100) and Stoke Hall Bridge (99), before winding into more open countryside. Beyond Vicker's Bridge (98), it is about half a mile to Hurleston Junction, and the

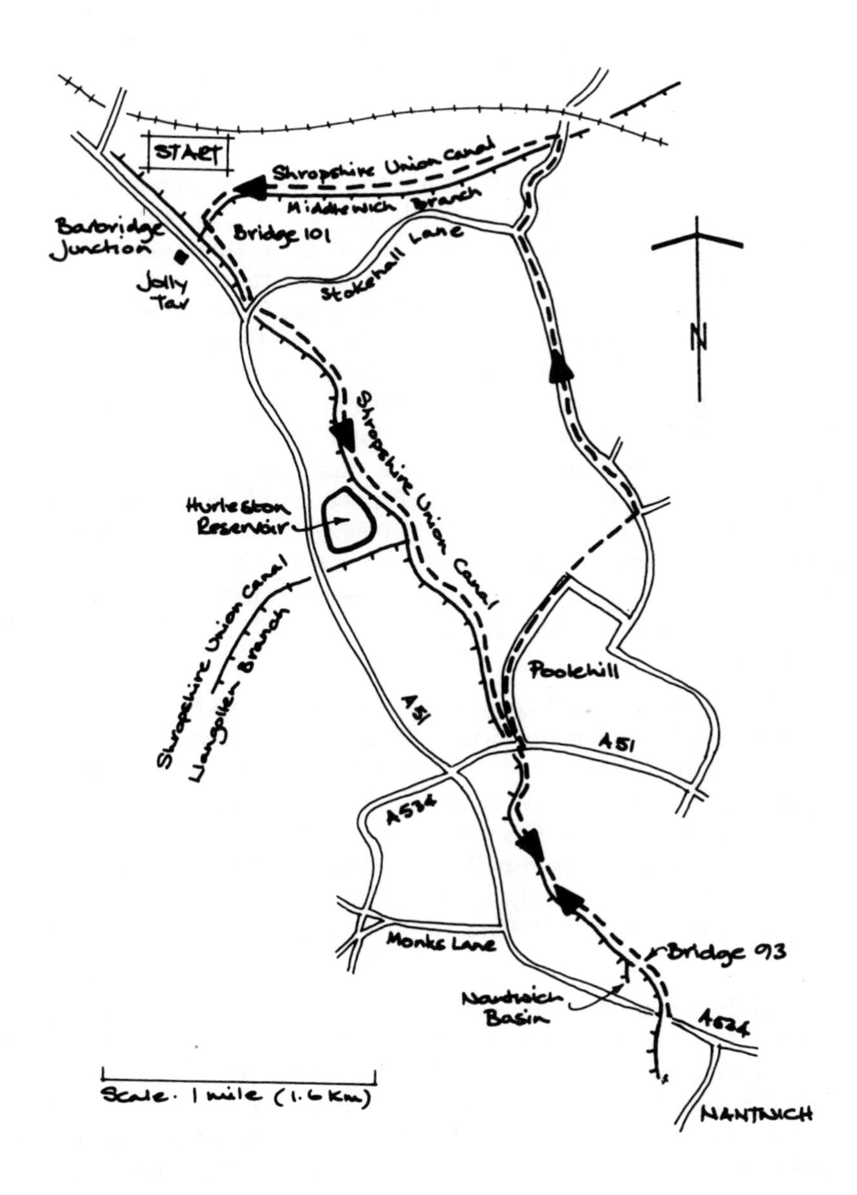
START
Shropshire Union Canal
Middlewich Branch
Barbridge Junction
Bridge 101
Jolly Tar
Stokehall Lane
N
Shropshire Union Canal
Hurleston Reservoir
Shropshire Union Canal
Llangollen Branch
Poolehill
A51
A51
A534
Monks Lane
Bridge 93
Nantwich Basin
A534
NANTWICH
Scale. 1 mile (1.6 Km)

Llangollen Canal. To the right, the four locks rear up steeply, raising the canal over 34ft on its way towards North Wales. After the junction, the Shropshire Union Canal follows its winding contour line under three bridges. This stretch is wide, with shallow edges where the bank has been eroded by cattle.

To return by a circular route, leave the canal at Henhull Bridge (95), where the A51 crosses the canal. At the bridge, turn left, then immediately left again into the narrow lane that runs parallel with the canal. Follow the lane for a mile, as it bends round to the right, and follow thge track up to Poole House Farm, and Oaktree Farm. The track runs along the right hand side of the farm buildings. Just beyond the second farm, it curves around to the left, after the junction with another path. The track becomes a path and, after crossing a stream, divides into two. Take the right fork, and follow it for a few hundred yards to where it joins a road. Follow the road for a mile and a quarter to where it forks. Again, take the right fork, and it is a couple of hundred yards to Cholmondeston Bridge, on the Middlewich Branch of the Shropshire Union Canal. Cross the canal, and join the towpath. Head left along the canal, and pass the lock. From here it is about a mile and a half back to Barbridge Junction, where the two canals meet, and the start of the walk.

To follow the linear walk, it is not far after bridge 95 to where the canal narrows by the remains of bridge 94. Soo after, there is a sharp bend, and the pretty 13th century church of St Mary's, Acton, comes into view on the right hand side. At Acton Bridge (93), a path leads off to the village. The church is well worth a visit, and there is also an attractive pub called The Star. About half a mile beyond Acton, there is Nantwich Basin, a long inlet on the right hand side, leading to British Waterways' boatyards, and to shops selling all kinds of canal souvenirs, as well as provisions.

Beyond the basin, the canal seems narrower, and Nantwich is the point where the wide Chester Canal heading north met the narrow Birmingham and Liverpool Canal leading south. While the former was built for use by wide-beamed Mersey flats, the latter was built for narrowboats with a maximum beam of 7ft. Surprisingly, the narrowboats, carrying cargoes of up to 25 tons, outlasted the much larger craft that navigated the northern section. The two waterways were amalgamated to form the Shropshire Union Canal in 1845. The Chester Canal is the older of the two, and it was opened in 1779. The Birmingham and Liverpool Canal, running from Nantwich to Autherley Junction, just north of Wolverhampton, was opened in 1835. Commercial traffic died out by the 1960s, and now the canal is exclusively used by pleasure craft.

Follow the towpath along the embankment, and the town of Nantwich appears on the left hand side. About a quarter of a mile beyond Nantwich Basin is Thomas Telford's cast iron aqueduct. Before it crosses the road, a set of steps lead down from the towpath. From here, it is about half a mile, to the left, to the centre of Nantwich. To get back to the start of the walk, turn around at this point. On the way back, it is fascinating to observe how the canal gradually widens, and the countryside opens out.

The old town of Nantwich is worth a visit. Like the other Cheshire 'wiches', Nantwich is a salt town, although the industry had died out by the end of the 19th century. Built on the banks of the River Weaver, Nantwich dates back to the Romans, but most of the town is Georgian or medieval. The splendid 13th century church of St Mary is remarkable for its octagonal tower. In 1583, during the reign of Elizabeth I, much of the town was so badly destroyed that the Queen herself provided funds for the re-building work. The noted herbalist, John Gerrard, came from Nantwich, and his book, written in 1597, contains the first ever picture of a potato! Opposite the church is the half-timbered Crown Hotel where, in the last century, a coachman known as Old Piggott (grandfather of Lester Piggott) used to work.

WALK 8: MIDDLEWICH BRANCH

Waterway: Middlewich Branch of the Shropshire Union Canal

Distance: 10 miles each way

Start: The junction of the Middlewich Branch with the Trent and Mersey Canal at Middlewich, beside the A533. Map reference: 706/657

Map: OS Pathfinder 775

How to get there: Start the walk just south of the town centre, where the A533 road to Sandbach crosses the canal. By bus from Northwich, take the E39 Middlewich circular service.

This is a linear walk, along one of the key links in the North West canal network, the Middlewich branch of the Shropshire Union Canal which connects the Trent and Mersey Canal with the main line of the Shropshire Union Canal. Although it is twenty miles to Barbridge and back, it is possible to walk the ten miles in one direction, and get back to the start by bus (or vice versa). There are many places where refreshments may be bought, and the towpath is in good condition the full length of the canal.

Start the walk from the junction of the Shropshire Union Canal's Middlewich branch with the Trent and Mersey Canal at Middlewich. From the town centre, head south on the A533 towards Sandbach. After about a quarter of a mile, the road crosses the canal.

The Walk:

Before crossing, join the canal towpath, and head right, away from the junction. Set into the bridge, there is a sign with 'Wardle Canal 1829' carved on it, and this is the old name for the Middlewich branch. It is also a reminder of the fact that the short stretch from the Trent and Mersey up to the first lock on the Middlewich Branch used to be no more than a small arm of the Trent and Mersey, before the rest of the canal was constructed.

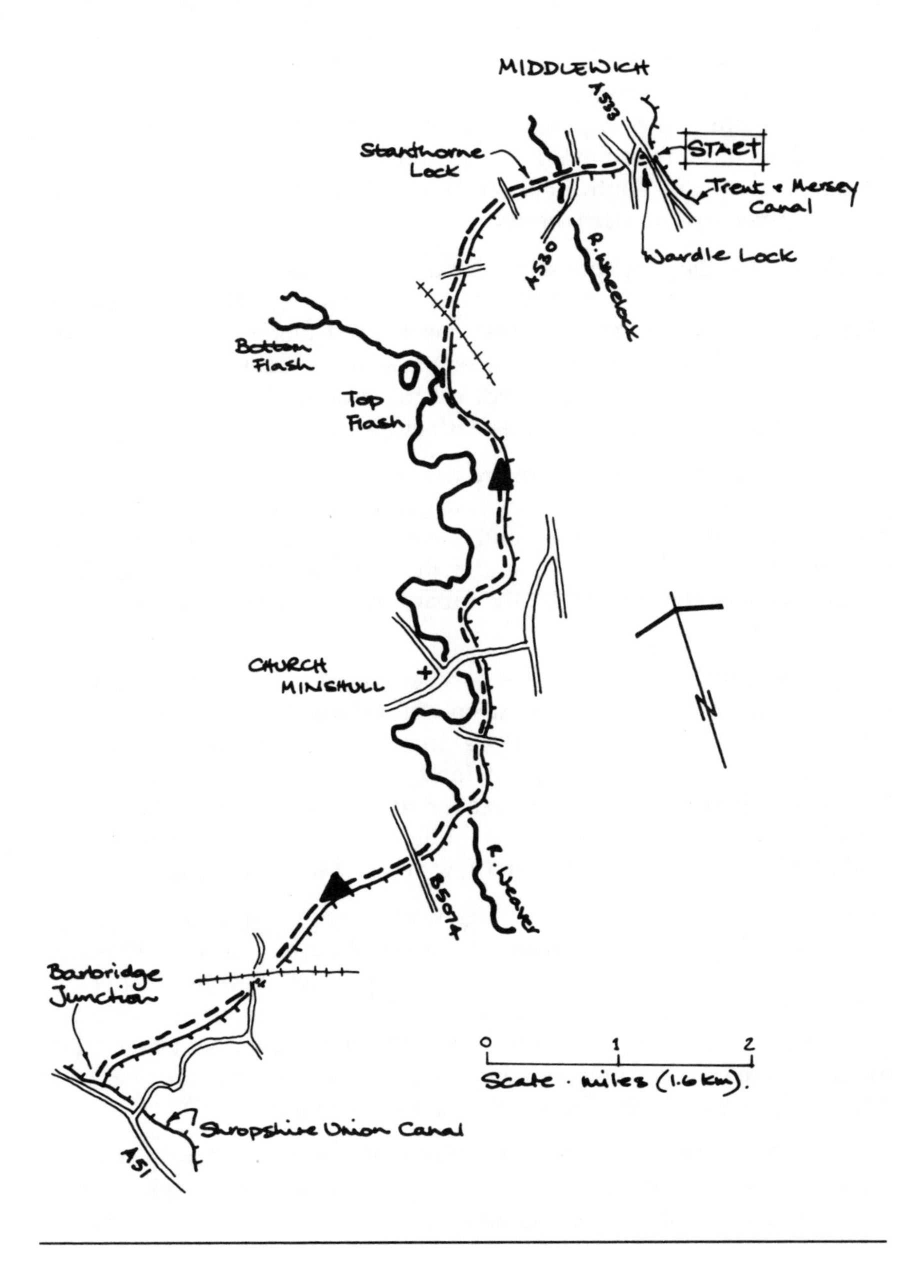
MIDDLEWICH
A533
START
Stanthorne Lock
Trent & Mersey Canal
Wardle Lock
A530
R. Wheelock
Bottom Flash
Top Flash
CHURCH MINSHULL
N
B5074
R. Weaver
Barbridge Junction
0
1
2
Scale · miles (1.6km).
Shropshire Union Canal
A51

Follow the towpath under three bridges, as the canal gradually winds its way out of Middlewich. After Court's Bridge (28), the canal is raised on an embankment to cross the River Wheelock, shortly before its confluence with the River Dane. Less than a quarter of a mile after the aqueduct, there is a bridge followed by Stanthorne Lock, which raises the canal up the side of the Wheelock valley. The canal winds around to the left to head due south. It passes through farming country, most of which is given over to dairy herds.

At bridge 22A, the canal passes under the main West Coast rail line. The Middlewich branch has an unusual connection with the railways. In 1888, a narrow gauge railway was constructed along the towpath, to investigate the possibility of using engines rather than horses to draw narrowboats. The scheme never got off the ground, but this method of navigation can still be seen on the continent today.

After Lea Hall Bridge (22), there are dramatic views to the right, across the Weaver Flashes, which are the furthest sections of the River Weaver that are navigable. The right hand bank of the canal is raised on an embankment as it curves to go under the two Twelve Acre Bridges (21 and 20). Shortly after bridge 20, the canal turns to the right, and enters a short cutting.

Along this section, the canal runs parallel with the River Weaver, soon looking down on it again from steep embankments. At bridge 14, the pretty village of Church Minshull is close by, to the right of the canal. The Badger Inn, there, serves good food, and is well worth a visit. The village is built around the River Weaver, and there is a weir which once provided power to operate the mill. The village church of St Bartholomew's was built in the first few years of the 18th century.

From bridge 14, the canal curves its way through cuttings and along embankments to where it crosses the River Weaver just after Prescott Bridge (10), by way of a three arched aqueduct. Beyond Nanney's Bridge (8) is Minshull Lock, rising the canal still further towards its junction with the main line of the Shropshire Union. Immediately after bridge 6 there is a thickly wooded cutting, and then the canal comes out at the bridge carrying the Crewe - Chester railway line.

On the other side is the busy boatyard of Venetian Marine, where souvenirs and refreshments can be bought. On the other side is the well-kept Cholmondeston Lock, and from here to Barbridge Junction, the canal runs through open countryside. There are four more bridges, then the canal comes to an end at the busy junction. The attractive Barbridge Inn, just to the left along the Shropshire Union, and on the far bank, serves Boddington's beers and good food. To return to the start of the walk, follow the towpath back if you have time. Otherwise, it is possible to catch a bus into Nantwich, then another from there to Middlewich (check times before starting the walk).

WALK 9: WHEELOCK TO HASSALL GREEN

Waterway: Trent and Mersey Canal

Distance: 5 miles

Start: Cheshire Cheese, Wheelock. Map reference: 751/593

Map: OS Pathfinder 791

How to get there: From Sandbach, take the A534 towards Crewe to where the road crosses the canal at Wheelock. By bus from Sandbach, take the K36 or K37 Crewe service.

This five mile walk passes the unusual double locks of the Trent and Mersey Canal, and the early stages of the River Wheelock, no more than six miles from its source on the sides of Mow Cop. Refreshments can be bought at several places en route.

The Walk:

Start the walk at The Cheshire Cheese, Wheelock, two miles south of Sandbach on the A534 towards Crewe. The road crosses over the Trent and Mersey Canal, and immediately after, on the left, is the Cheshire Cheese pub, which sells Tetley's beer. Just before the pub, a track leads past Wheelock Wharf to the canal towpath. Follow this, and head along the path away from the pub. The canal bends to the right, and it is raised above the low-lying Wheelock valley, with an aqueduct crossing the River Wheelock. Soon after, there is one of the iron mile posts that are a common sight on the Trent and Mersey, and it reads Preston Brook 23 miles, Shardlow 69. The canal can be drained into pastures on the right hand side, by way of sluices set against the towpath.

A hundred yards after the mile post, there is a double bridge leading into one of the Trent and Mersey's distinctive double locks, built to speed up traffic along the waterway. This is the first of the Wheelock flight of eight locks which raise the canal a total of 79ft 6ins. Just before the bridge, the canal crosses one of the many small streams feeding the

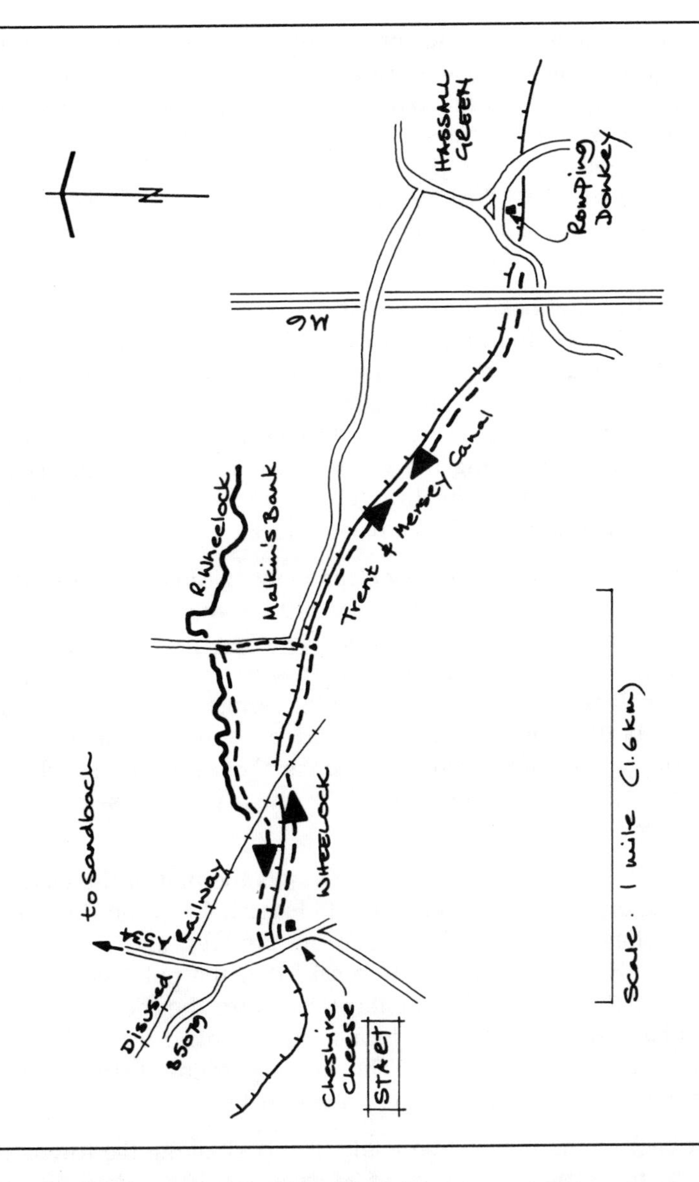

River Wheelock. Soon after the lock (66), there is a narrow pound which has been widened on the opposite bank to increase the volume of water supplying the lock, and another double lock (65).

The canal heads under the bridge of the now disused Northwich to Stoke railway line. After the bridge, the canal swings round to the right, and the village of Malkin's Bank appears dead ahead. On the right hand side, there is a golf course. Lock 64, another double, is particularly well-kept, and is soon followed by 63. An interesting feature of these double locks is that, directly below the bottom gates, there are narrow wooden footbridges across the chamber which are split to allow a tow rope through.

Shortly after the lock, the towpath crosses the entrance to a boatyard, and on the other side houses back onto the canal. A couple of hundred yards after the boatyard, there are the remains of a double lock. The left hand lock still works, but the one on the right has had its gates removed, and the lock chamber has been filled in with a series of sloping planes, cascading the water down from the upper pound. It is not far to a low, dripping bridge, and lock 61. On the bottom gates, there is a warning that this is a narrow lock.

Beyond lock 61, there is a very clear view of Mow Cop, in the distance to the left of the canal. After bridge 149 are the remaining two locks of the Wheelock flight. The last time I walked past lock 60, the pound above it had been drained, and repair work was taking place. Without the water, it was possible to see the workings of the paddles, and how the clay bottom of the canal formed a central channel. It was also reassuring to see how well-kept the canal was. Beyond lock 59, which was largely reconstructed in 1988, the canal goes under the M6 motorway.

Almost immediately after the motorway is the first of the Hassall Green locks. The bridge just beyond leads to Hassall Green on the left. There is a good village shop, which is open on Sundays, and an attractive pub called The Romping Donkey. It is said that the pub, which used to be called The Rampant Lion, got its name from the fact that its inn sign was so badly-painted that the locals said it looked more like a romping donkey than a rampant lion. The pub's gardens overlook the pound above the second of Hassall Green's two locks.

To get back to the start of the walk, turn back along the towpath. In the distance, the square tower of St Mary's Sandbach, designed by Giles Gilbert Scott in the mid 19th century, is clearly visible. Immediately after lock 63, cross over the bridge to the opposite side of the canal.

Follow the road to where it comes out at a T-junction. Turn left into Hassall Road and follow the road downhill for about a quarter of a mile. Just before crossing the fast-flowing River Wheelock, there is a stile leading off to the left. Cross over, and follow the river - there is no path to speak of. Alongside the river, there are meadows with willow trees and numerous low shrubs.

The river twists and turns, and it is important to keep an eye open for a railway arch to the left. It is less than half a mile after the stile, but all too easily missed. When the arch comes into view, follow the edge of the field leading up to it. Through the arch, there is a stile leading into a field. There is no clear path, so aim for the metal gate at the other side of the field. Beside it, there is a wooden stile to the left of it leading onto a track. Fifty yards further on, the track comes out by the canal and lock 66.

Carry on past the lock to the bridge. Before crossing over, there is a stile leading to the opposite bank from the towpath. Climb over, and follow the edge of the canal. Beside the aqueduct over the River Wheelock, there is a deep, murky pool to the right. The path finally comes out by a set of steps leading up to the bridge across the canal at Wheelock.

WALK 10: KING'S LOCK TO WHATCROFT

Waterway: Trent and Mersey Canal

Distance: 3 miles each way, or 7 miles by a circular route.

Start: King's Lock, Middlewich, beside the A533. Map reference: 706/657

Map: OS Pathfinder 775

How to get there: The walk starts just to the south of Middlewich town centre on the A533 towards Sandbach. By bus from Northwich, take the E39 Middlewich circular service.

This is a linear walk, of about three miles in each direction, but can be extended into a circular route. It gives a good impression of how the Trent and Mersey Canal has evolved since its construction in the latter half of the 18th century. There is a well-kept towpath for the whole of the walk, and refreshments can be bought in Middlewich.

The Walk:

Start the walk just to the south of Middlewich at King's Lock. Heading south from Middlewich on the A533 toward Sandbach, the Trent and Mersey Canal is to the left of the road. Soon after crossing the Shropshire Union Canal, the canal runs right alongside the road, and the first lock is King's Lock, with the King's Lock pub beside it. Join the footpath, which runs between the road and the canal, and head back in the direction of Middlewich. King's Lock is narrow, but very deep, dropping the canal by ten feet. Go under the bridge, and it is a short distance to the bridge over the entrance to the Shropshire Union Canal. This is a busy junction, especially since it is the starting point for many holiday makers on the canal.

Stay on the Trent and Mersey, and go under bridge 169. On the other side, there are the three Middlewich locks which, between them, drop the canal by over 30 ft to pass through the town centre. One of the

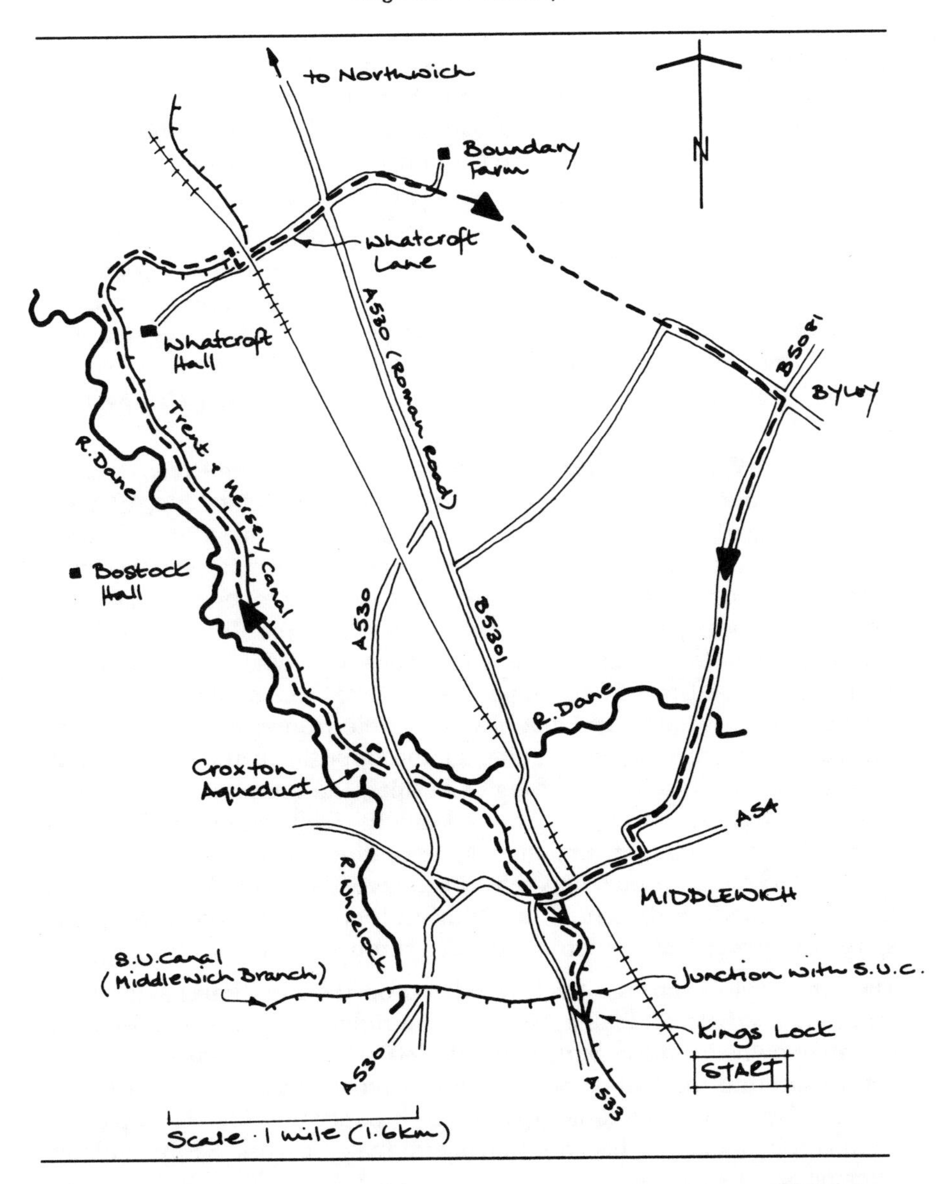

Cheshire salt towns, the Romans, aptly enough, named Middlewich 'Salinae'. The town's prosperity also owes much to the canal network, which provided transport links to distribute salt and brine throughout the country. It is an old town, and the library contains examples of

Stone Age weapons and Roman pottery. In 1642, one of the battles of the Civil War took place at Middlewich. St Michael's Church, with its imposing tower and its medieval stocks, offered refuge to the Royalist troops, who were defeated by the Parliament forces of William Brereton.

After lock 74, the canal passes under bridge 170, making its way north. It is just under half a mile to Middlewich Big Lock. This is a wide lock, with a rise of only 5ft. It marks the start of the wide, lock-free section of the canal which runs as far as the junction with the Bridgewater Canal at Preston Brook. At one time, the larger salt boats navigated this stretch, but when Croxton Aqueduct had to be replaced, a narrow channel was built which put paid to any craft wider than 7ft travelling north.

After the lock, the curiously-named River Croco joins the River Dane on the right hand side of the canal, and the Dane runs close by. After the road bridge (173), it is only a few hundred yards to the Croxton Aqueduct. This narrow trestle structure carries the canal over the River Dane. The wooden towpath, and the lack of any stonework make the aqueduct appear particularly precarious. Beneath, the River Dane flows quickly, towards its confluence with the River Wheelock. From this point, the River Dane flows alongside the canal for the next two miles, although it is wooded and not always visible from the towpath. After bridge 175, there is a wide bulge in the opposite bank of the canal. Along much of its journey through Cheshire, the Trent and Mersey has been affected by subsidence caused by the salt industry. This has resulted in numerous diversions and re-routings, with the old line left as little more than a puzzling relic. In the woods on the left hand side, there is Bostock Hall School, an 18th century former mansion whose spires and towers can sometimes be seen through the trees.

The canal passes through thick woodland on the right hand side. After bridge 178, Whatcroft Hall appears on the right hand side, a substantial privately-owned house built around 1800. The canal curves ninety degrees around the hall, almost forming a moat. It was here that James Brindley, who built the canal, redesigned a paper mill for his employer, Abraham Bennet, who had been unable to make it work. Sadly, nothing remains of it today.

In 1765, a pamphlet was published by the famous potter, Josiah Wedgwood, 'A View of the Advantages of Inland Navigation, with a Plan of a Navigable Canal intended for Communication between the

Ports of Liverpool and Hull'. Although Brindley preferred to refer to the canal as the Grand Trunk Canal, it is more commonly known as the Trent and Mersey. Work began in 1766, and the canal was completed, five years after Brindley's death, in 1777.

From Whatcroft Hall, the route back to the start of the walk is to head back along the towpath. For a slightly longer, circular route, cross over the canal just beyond Whatcroft Hall by bridge 179. On the far side of the bridge, a path leads off to the left. Follow the path to where it joins a narrow lane. Turn left into the lane, and it is just under a mile to where it meets the Roman Road of King Street, the A530. Turn left and, almost immediately, a track leads off on the opposite side of the road. After quarter of a mile, the track bends to the right. It becomes a less distinct path for the next quarter of a mile or so, to where it comes out on the left hand side of Drakelow Hall Farm. Follow the farm drive for the half mile to, where it joins a minor road. Turn left, and follow the road as it bends round to the right, leading to the small village of Byley with its large church and little else.

The Trent and Mersey Canal at Middlewich

At the crossroads in the centre of the village, turn right, following the B5081 for about two miles into Middlewich. The road crosses the River Dane, and comes out at the main A54. Turn right, and it is about a quarter of a mile to where it crosses the Trent and Mersey Canal. Join the towpath, heading to the left, and it is about a quarter of a mile back to King's Lock and the start of the walk.

WALK 11: MARSTON TO BARNTON

Waterway: Trent and Mersey Canal

Distance: 3 miles each way

Start: Bridge 193, Marston. Map reference: 671/755

Map: OS Pathfinder 758

How to get there: From Northwich, take the A559 towards Warrington, then turn into the B5075 to Marston. By bus from Northwich, take the X2 Knutsford service.

This is a linear walk which shows the effects of the salt industry upon the waterways, passes through both industrial and rural landscapes, and passes the unique Anderton Boat lift. The walk can be extended by leaving the canal at bridge 196, crossing over it and entering the richly-wooded Marbury Country Park.

To start the walk, take the A559 Warrington to Lostock Gralam road. Heading south, take a road to the right, about a mile after the Great Budworth crossroad; heading north, take the next left after the road to Wincham. After passing two ponds, on either side, the road goes up to the Trent and Mersey Canal. On the other side is Marston and 'The Salt Barge', an attractive little pub which also sells food.

The Walk:

From the bridge (193), there is a slope down to the towpath on the right hand side. Follow the towpath away from the bridge. Marston is no more than a hamlet, but is famous for its old salt mines. Despite new methods of extracting salt, so much has already been mined beneath Marston that the village is gradually sinking as the remaining salt dissolves. It has been recorded that, in 1844, Tsar Nicholas I of Russia visited Marston to see its mines workings and dined with members of the Royal Society actually inside the ancient salt mine, which is over 350 feet deep and covers 35 acres.

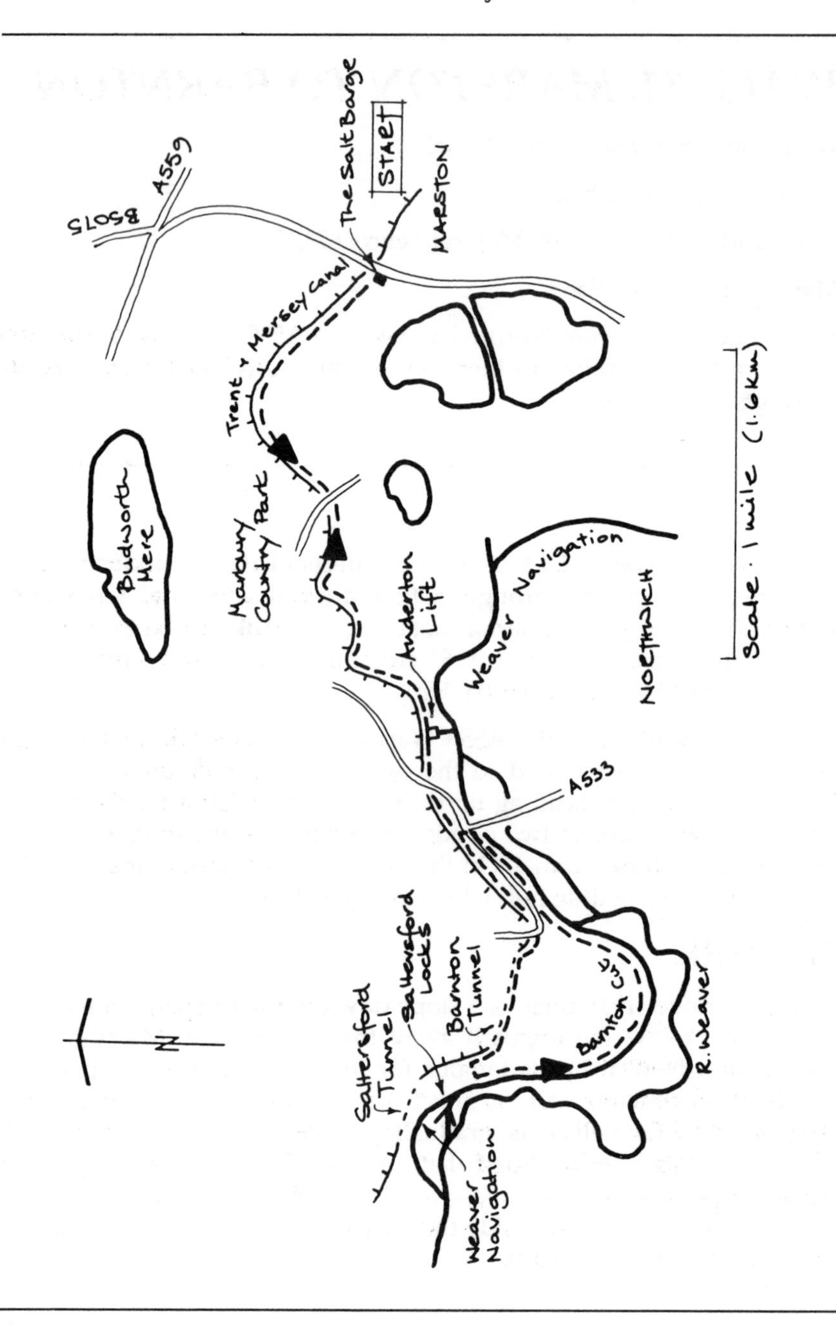
B5075
A559
The Salt Barge
START
MARSTON
Trent & Mersey Canal
Budworth Mere
Marbury Country Park
Anderton Lift
Weaver Navigation
NORTHWICH
A533
Scale · 1 mile (1.6km)
Saltersford Tunnel
Saltersford Locks
Barnton Tunnel
Barnton Cut
R. Weaver
Weaver Navigation
N

To the left, there are two very large reservoirs nestling in a loop between the Weaver Navigation's Witton Brook branch and the Trent and Mersey. This stretch of canal is one of the most recent additions to the navigation. Known as Marston New Cut, this is a half-mile section of the canal which was opened in 1958. It was constructed, at some speed, as a diversion when it was found that the canal was in danger of being swallowed up by a collapsing mine shaft. Within two months of the new cut being opened, a crater, formed by the shaft, did indeed extend into the canal bed of the old line.

In the distance, to the right is the square sandstone tower of Great Budworth church. This is one of Cheshire's prettiest villages, and well worth a detour. Within a mile, the canal turns almost ninety degrees to the left. Beyond the bend, the canal goes into attractive, wooded countryside. It crosses Forge Brook, a pretty stream that winds its way down from Budworth Mere, through Marbury Country Park, via a small pond on the left of the canal, and down to the Weaver Navigation.

Follow the towpath under bridge 196, which carries the road through Marbury Country Park. The canal crosses another brook, Marbury or Cogshall Brook which used to power the mill on the estate owned by William Marbury, then goes under the canal to join the Weaver. Over the next half mile, the canal goes under two bridges, winding through two ninety degree bends, then opens out in the stretch up to the Anderton Lift. The old boat lift, which is being renovated, is on the left. The land falls away steeply to the left, down to the Weaver and its rows of chemical wharves on the far bank.

In order for the Weaver to develop a greater amount of traffic from the Bridgewater Canal, a junction with the Trent and Mersey Canal was planned at Anderton. The idea of a hydraulic boat lift came from Edward Leader Williams, and it was finally opened in July 1875, raising boats over fifty feet from the Weaver to the Trent and Mersey. Construction of the lift was not helped by problems of subsidence, caused by salt mining in the area. This increased the cost of the lift, and there were to be amendments not long after it was opened as, in 1882, there was a burst, and a barge fell to the bottom of the lift.

Beyond the Anderton Lift, the towpath overlooks Winnington Weir on the Weaver. This takes the old line of the River Weaver to the south of the navigation, before joining it again two miles further on, below

Saltersford Locks. The level of Winnington Weir was raised in 1859, after Northwich Lock was removed. Beside the weir are the giant chemical works of ICI. Apart from a short stretch of stonework, there is little evidence of Winnington Lock, demolished towards the end of the last centrury. By raising the level by about four feet at Saltersford Locks, further downstream, it was possible to do away with Winnington Lock. Although few rail links were built with the Weaver's wharves, Winnington did have an exchange wharf which was widely used in the second half of the 19th century.

The Anderton Boat Lift

Shortly after bridge 200, the A533 Northwich to Runcorn road runs alongside for nearly half a mile before crossing the Trent and Mersey Canal. Just beyond, is the start of Barnton Tunnel which is 572 yards long. The narrow, curving tunnel has no towpath and in the days of horse drawn boats, was navigated by legging - lying on the top of the boat, and pushing against the rock of the tunnel with one's feet. This tunnel, and Saltersford further on were the first to be built, taking a commercial waterway through, rather than over raised country. At this point, the canal is about 80 feet above sea level, with land to the north rising steeply.

Immediately beyond the entrance to Barnton Tunnel, the countryside is not particulary attractive, but the enthusiast may be interested in following the track above Barnton tunnel to the the point where it bends to the right, down to the Weaver Navigation. By turning left and following the Barnton cut section of the Weaver, constructed in 1771, it is possible to work one's way back to where the A533 runs between the Weaver and the Trent and Mersey canal, and from there follow the towpath along the canal back to Marston. When the Weaver Valley Way is complete, and the whole of the river's towpath has been restored, it will be possible to follow the Weaver as far as Anderton, and join the Trent and Mersey towpath there, above the boatlift.

Otherwise, the entrance to Barnton Tunnel marks the end of the linear route, and the route back to Marston is along the towpath. Just before the Weaver curves round to meet the road, one passes Barnton Weir, near where Barnton Lock once stood. This serves as an overflow, taking excess water from the navigation to the old line of the Weaver.

WALK 12: DUTTON

Waterways: River Weaver, Trent and Mersey Canal

Distance: 5 miles

Start: Acton Bridge swing bridge on the A49. Map reference: 601/761

Map: OS Pathfinder 758

How to get there: From junction 10 on the M56, it is six miles south along the A49 to the swing bridge. By bus from Northwich, take the E47 or E48 Frodsham services to just south of the swing bridge on the A49.

This walk is about five miles in length, and takes in a section of the River Weaver which can be followed without having to wear waders, and a high level stretch of the Trent and Mersey Canal. These are two very different waterways: a river that has been canalised (although several loops of the old river still remain) to form the Weaver Navigation, and a narrow canal, originally part of a plan to link Liverpool and Hull by a commercial waterway.

The Walk:

Start the walk from the A49 swing bridge over the Weaver. It is about six miles south of the junction (10) between the M56 and the A49. At the bridge, head west along a well-made track. The Weaver is to the left and, a little beyond the bridge, one can look back and see the old line of the river branching away from the navigation. On the right is a steepish embankment made from earth dug out in creating the navigation, and this has become a favourite haunt of wading birds.

The conversion of the Weaver into a navigable waterway began in the early 18th century, to provide an easy way of bringing coal to fuel the Cheshire salt industry. Of the original twelve locks that were constructed, only five deep locks exist today, although the remains of Pickering's Lock and Frodsham Lock are still clearly visible.

The track follows the Weaver as it bends northward. Although the navigation is wide and slow-moving, the tree-lined ridge beyond the

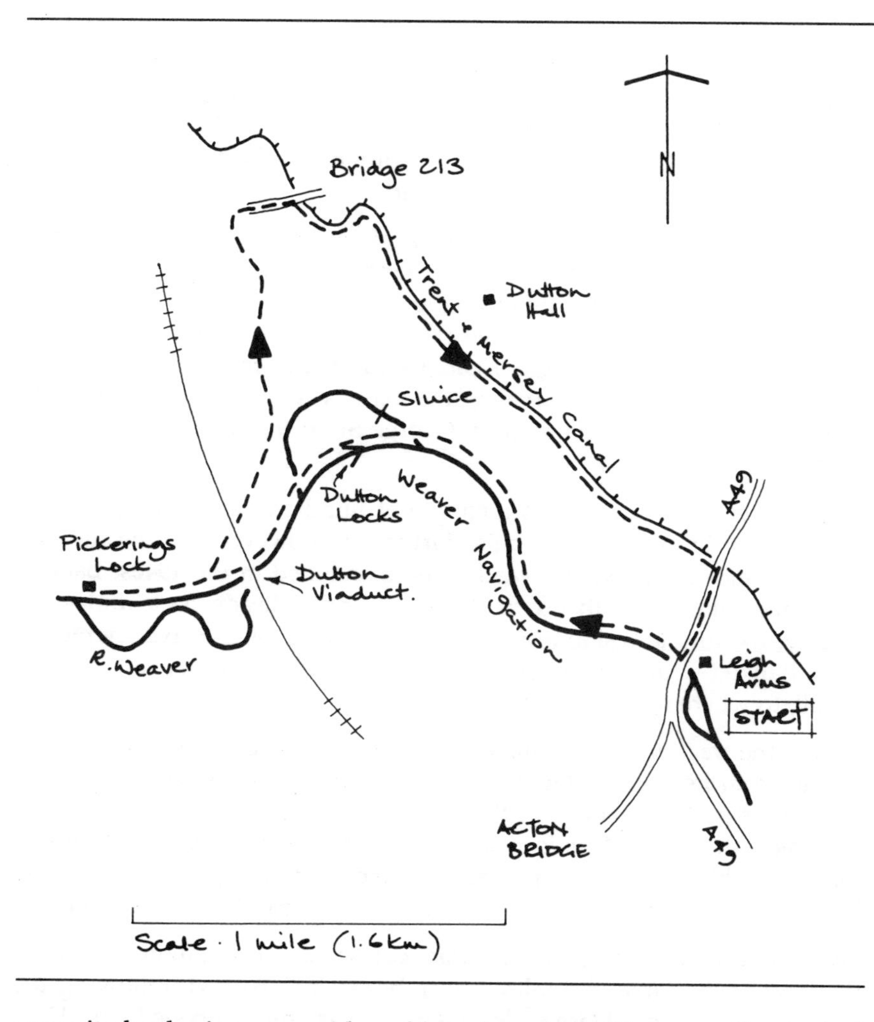

opposite bank gives some idea of how broad the Weaver valley is, and how substantial the river must once have been.

The Weaver bends west again, and Dutton Locks come into view. The navigation forks at this point. Over the right hand branch is a white wooden footbridge. This is the old line of the river and, just beyond the footbridge, its progress is blocked by Dutton Sluices - a weir that can be controlled to regulate the water level.

Crossing the footbridge, one comes to the left hand branch which leads into the locks. There are two parallel locks, one larger than the other so that, when smaller craft want to pass through, they do not use up more water than is necessary. The original lock keeper's cottages are on the north side of the locks. On the opposite side, there is the macabre sight of a pair of legs (belonging to a tailor's dummy) fully clothed and shod, coming out of an old set of winding gear!

After the locks, the old line of the river rejoins the navigation, so that an island is formed where the cottages stand. The thoughtful lock keeper has put up a list of the different nationalities of ships that have passed through Dutton Locks. Follow the path down, past the locks, and cross over another white footbridge. Dead ahead are the impressive sandstone arches of Dutton viaduct, carrying the main west coast rail line over the Weaver. The viaduct was built by George Stephenson, and was opened in 1837.

Once under the viaduct, it is a couple of hundred yards to a path that leads off to the right. A half mile further on, however, are the remains of Pickering's Lock, which was finally abandoned in the 1940s. Back to the walk, take the path off to the right, and it heads back under the viaduct to run alongside a land-locked old loop of the river, which is often flanked with anglers. The path curves gradually to the left, slightly uphill, to where it meets a good track.

Follow the track to a junction, and turn right. It is less than a quarter of a mile from here to bridge 213 over the Trent and Mersey Canal. The towpath is on the nearside of the bridge. Turn right, and head eastward alongside the canal. This is near the northern end of the canal, and it follows a high contour line, above, and running parallel with the Weaver, until the two are joined by the historic boat lift at Anderton.

The Trent and Mersey Canal was cut at the instigation of Josiah Wedgwood, by James Brindley. Work began in 1766 and, following the completion of the Harecastle Tunnel, was fully opened in 1777. Formerly known as the Grand Trunk Canal, the Trent and Mersey is over 93 miles long with 76 locks.

Following the canal, there are splendid views across the Weaver valley. After just under two miles, one comes across a boatyard on the right, just before the bridge where the A49 crosses the canal. Turning right at the main road, it is only a couple of hundred yards back to the swing bridge and the start of the walk.

Acton Swing Bridge

In the short stretch of road between the two waterways, there are three attractive pubs where one can get refreshments. Just to the north of the Trent and Mersey is the 'Holly Bush', a delightfully unspoilt pub with a thatched roof and a pretty garden, and further down towards the swing bridge are 'The Horns' and 'Leigh Arms', both of which offer a good choice of food.

WALK 13: ACTON BRIDGE TO SALTERSFORD

Waterways: River Weaver, Trent and Mersey Canal

Distance: $4^1/_2$ miles

Start: Acton Bridge swing bridge on the A49. Map reference: 601/761

Map: OS Pathfinder 758

How to get there: From junction 10 on the M56, it is six miles south on the A49 to the swing bridge. By bus from Northwich, take the E47, or E48 services to just south of the swing bridge on the A49.

This is a short walk, being only 4 miles, but it can be a muddy one. The Weaver does not have the well-kept towpaths of the narrow canals, and there are some stretches where the paths are hard to make out, being quite badly overgrown. The Weaver holds a special attraction for me, and if one wants to extend this walk, it can easily be joined onto the walk between Dutton and Acton Bridge.

The Walk:

The walk begins from the Acton Bridge swing bridge where the A49 crosses the Weaver. The bridge is about six miles south of the A49's junction with the M56. To the left of the bridge is the Leigh Arms. Take the path, down to the towpath, to the left of the bridge. Follow the towpath and a little way after joining it, there is the raised stone work which is all that remains of Acton Bridge Lock, built in the 1730s. It was removed in the last century during efforts made to streamline the navigation.

Beyond the other bank, there is the old course of the river which joins the navigation shortly after the lock channel. The old course is full of moored craft. The path comes to a stile and on the other side, follows a line of telegraph poles. Near the junction with the old course, the opposite bank becomes more built up: houses with gardens sloping down to the bank, and a restaurant called 'The Rhinegold'. The path

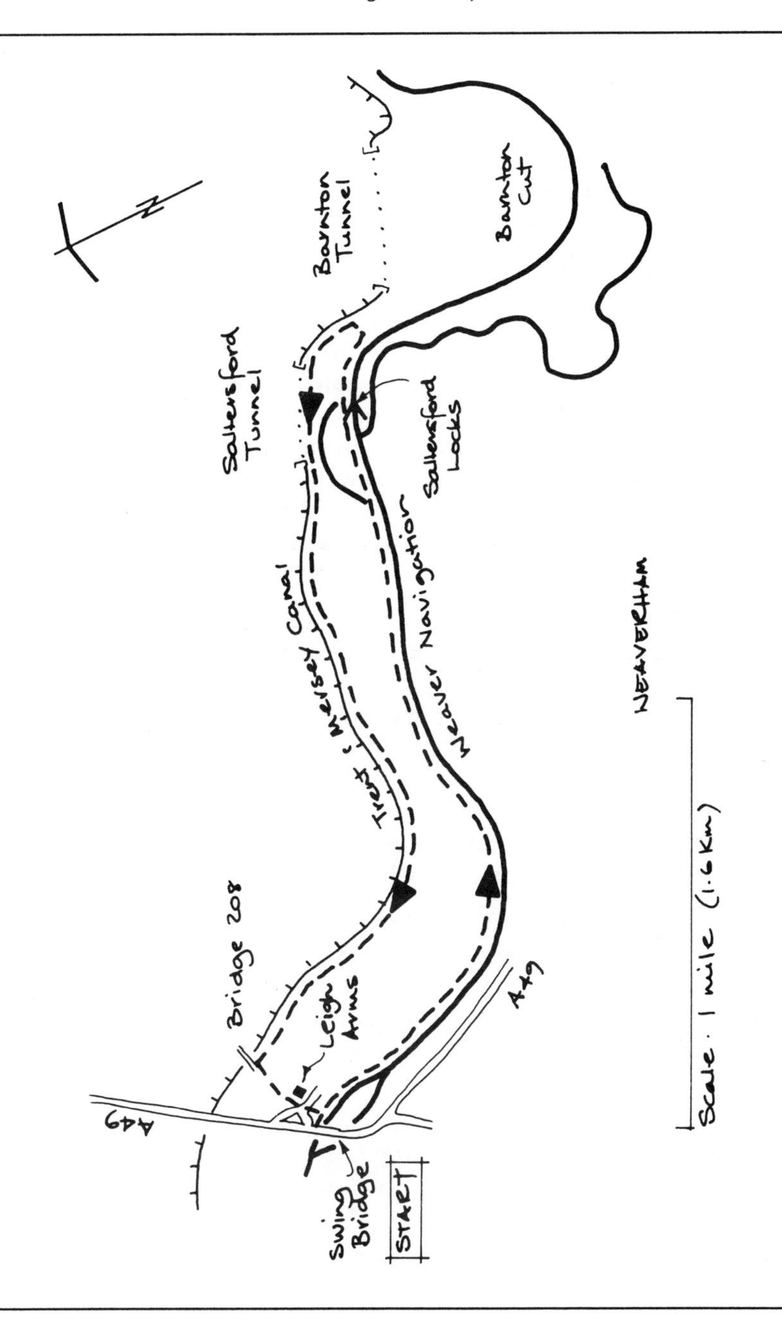
Barnton Cut
Barnton Tunnel
Saltersford Tunnel
Saltersford Locks
Trent & Mersey Canal
Weaver Navigation
WEAVERHAM
Bridge 208
Leigh Arms
A49
Swing Bridge
START
Scale: 1 mile (1.6 Km)
N

joins a well-made track. Keep following the Weaver as the opposite bank becomes thickly wooded.

Go through a gate, and the path becomes less defined as the Weaver swings gradually round to the left. Beyond the next stile, the path is better, and is slightly raised above the field beside it. There are often heifers in this field. They tend to be rather inquisitive, but harmless. After the next stile, the Weaver appears less channelled, winding from side to side like a river until Saltersford Locks come into view. There is woodland up the slopes to the left, while the square sandstone tower of Weaverham Church is clearly visible to the right. The church, dedicated to St Mary the Virgin, dates back to the 15th century, yet it is on the site of two previous churches. There was a Saxon church mentioned in the Domesday Book, which was later run by the monks from Vale Royal Abbey. The second church was complete by the latter half of the 14th century. The path follows the edge of a field to a line of poplars which lead to a white footbridge. This stretch was full of yellowhammers the last time I visited it.

The white footbridge crosses the weir channel, and leads to an island where the Saltersford lock keeper has his cottage. The channel is a very quiet backwater, although a steady flow comes down it from the sluices. On the opposite bank, the old course runs off, just before the locks. It carries on for almost three miles until re-joining the navigation further upstream at Winnington. To avoid the tight bends and sandbanks along this stretch, the Barnton Cut was built just beyond the locks between 1832 and 1835, replacing a previous cut, made in 1771. The mouth of the old course is now a home for elderly barges.

The locks are Saltersford, like most to be found along the Weaver, are in a remote location, and there is a certain grandeur in the way they channel and control the Weaver. The lock keeper has put up a panel of photographs showing some of the ships which have used the lock, and there is even one of the Royal Navy using the navigation. Perhaps they took a wrong turning at Liverpool!

Follow the path along the left side of the locks to the sluices which are set in what was presumably the old lock channel before the double locks were constructed in 1848-9. Another bridge crosses the weir channel, and leads to a tarmac track. On the opposite bank of the Weaver, there is a steep overflow leading down to the old course. Just before the track bends, the path beside the Weaver leads off to the right. It is possible to follow the navigation for about another mile, until the path comes out at the more industrial landscape between Winnington and the eastern end of the Trent and Mersey Canal's Barnton Tunnel.

For the purposes of this walk, however, follow the tarmac track uphill as it curves to the left, away from the Weaver. At the top, there is the Trent and Mersey Canal. Turn left onto the towpath, beside where the canal forms a wide basin, built for craft queueing to enter Saltersford Tunnel to the left, or Barnton Tunnel to the right. From this 'clearing' between the tunnels, there is a splendid view across the Weaver to Frodsham Hill. The canal curves gently to enter Salterford Tunnel.

There is no towpath through the tunnel, and the path leads up the left hand side of the entrance to the roof. There is a plaque to commemorate the re-opening of the tunnel in 1984 (by Sir Frank Price, Chairman of British Waterways Board) after major repairs. It is pitch black inside the tunnel and, since it follows a crooked line, it seems an inordinately long time before the dot of light at the other end comes into view. At the top of the tunnel entrance, the path turns left, following the line of the canal. Follow the path uphill. It soon becomes very wooded, with steep banks sloping away to the left. Just before a gate, there is one of the canal's milestones: Preston Brook (where it meets the Bridgewater) 5 miles, Shardlow (where it meets the River Trent) 87 miles. After the gate, head downhill, until the path comes out at the other end of the 424 yard tunnel. This is a particularly pretty stretch of the Trent and Mersey, with excellent views to the left. The Weaver is about sixty feet below, and the canal keeps at this level as far as Preston Brook.

Soon after passing under the brick and iron of bridge 204, the canal narrows to cross an aqueduct, leading over a brook and a track. After the white brick bridge (206), the canal heads into more open country. In several sections, it is quite wide with thick reed beds along the opposite bank. This stretch is often lined with anglers who try to lure out the inhabitants of these reed beds. Go under bridge 208, then up the side of it. Turn right onto a path leading away from the bridge. It is very overgrown, but after thirty yards there is a stile which leads onto a better path along the edge of a field. Cross another stile, and there is a fenced path that leads back to the Leigh Arms and the swingbridge at Acton Bridge.

Canal Notes:

The Weaver is THE salt river, passing through the heart of Cheshire, with its lop-sided towns undermined by centuries of salt mining and brine extraction. The names on towns and villages along the river reflect this heritage. The river joins the Manchester Ship Canal at Saltport, and there is the set of locks at Saltersford. In fact, the Romans even named nearby Middlewich 'Salinae'. The development of the Weaver navigation is filled with controversies that relate not surprisingly, to the salt industry. Producers of rock salt needed a cheap means of transportation, while brine men sought a cheap method of bringing in coal, as well as sending out the refined white salt produced from brine.

Despite stiff opposition from local landowners, who feared a decrease in value of farming land, work began in the first half of the 18th century to make the Weaver navigable. Locks were built at Acton Bridge and Saltersford, among the eleven that made the Weaver navigable to Winsford. Over the next fifty years a programme of improvements was carried out, and included the building of a new lock at Saltersford in 1762, and a new one at Acton Bridge in 1778.

The last section of the Trent and Mersey canal to be finished, north of Middlewich, was opened in 1777. This part of the canal runs more or less parallel to the Weaver and over the next few years, took a substantial proportion of trade away from it. Before the end of the 18th century, the expansion of the salt trade ensured that the navigation not only recovered, but handled a greater tonnage than ever before.

Today, it seems hard to imagine that canal boats were once hauled by men. Following the construction of a towpath along the Weaver from Frodsham to Anderton in the 1790s, the job was done by horses. With the increase in traffic on the navigation, it became necessary both to build double locks, and to deepen the Weaver. In 1844, Acton Bridge Lock was extended to 88ft by 18ft, and by 1857, there were double locks at Acton Bridge and Saltersford, as well as at Pickerings and Winnington. The larger of the two locks in these double locks, were 100ft long by 22ft and could take craft carrying well over 100 tons.

One of the recommendations, made in 1865, by Edward Leader Williams, was that it would be practicable to make the river navigable for sea-going vessels. The Weaver was given a minimum depth of 12ft, and there were plans to make the locks larger still. By the early 1870s, salt trade had exceeded a million tons. In the last quarter of the 19th century, Saltersford Locks were extended to 220′ by 42′ 6″, and Acton Bridge Lock was removed. Today, freighters with up to 1000 tonnes deadweight capacity pass along the navigation. The most recent improvement along this stretch of the Weaver is the A49 Swing bridge at Acton Bridge. Built in 1933, it weighs 650 tons, although the greater part of this is supported by a floating pontoon.

WALK 14: HUNT'S LOCKS TO VALE ROYAL

Waterway: River Weaver

Distance: 6 miles

Start: Riverside Park, Northwich. Map reference: 653/728

Map: OS Pathfinder 758

How to get there: Take the A559 out of Northwich towards Hartford, turn right into Darwin Street, which becomes Lower Darwin Street, then follow the road downhill to where Riverside branches off to the right. By bus from Northwich, take the C89 Tarporley service, get off on the A559 and follow Darwin Street down to the start of the walk.

This is a walk with everything: contrasts between urban and rural, a natural river that shows feats of engineering to make it navigable, splendid scenery, and a remarkable history.

Northwich is at the heart of the Cheshire salt industry and the development of the Weaver Navigation is all about salt. By the early 18th century, the production of salt relied on coal fired heat, rather than wood. Getting Lancashire coal south was no easy task, involving pack horses, boats and a convoluted journey. Similarly, no cheap means of transport was available for distributing large volumes of unrefined rock salt.

The walk is about six miles long. With broad towpaths for much of the way, it is more sociable than some, as one does not have to spend the whole walk in single file. Although not a particularly strenuous walk, it can easily be extended to form a rather longer one by continuing on the towpath beyond Vale Royal Locks. It is possible to follow this section of the Weaver, the Vale Royal Cut, for another two and half miles to the bridge at Bradford Mill. Beyond the locks, however, there is only a towpath on the one side so getting back means crossing the bridge, turning right and following the road to Whitegate for a mile and half before getting onto the path that leaves the right hand side of the road, and takes one down to the opposite side of Vale Royal Locks. The alternative is to double back to the locks.

Hunt's Locks

To start the walk, head for the centre of Northwich. From there, take the A559 towards Hartford and Chester. The road passes a large church with a spire on the left, and the fifth street on the left after this is Darwin Street. Follow the street downhill, it goes under a railway bridge, and becomes Lower Darwin Street. Go straight across the two small roundabouts that follow, and the road leading off the second, Riverside Park curves away to the right, where one can park.

The Walk:

Follow Riverside Park for about 20 yards, and there is a set of steps leading down to the left. It soon becomes a grassy path through trees. It bears to the left, up to the river's raised banks. Follow the edge of the river heading left, and one comes to Hunt's Locks. Beyond are the imposing arches of the viaduct carrying the Chester to Manchester

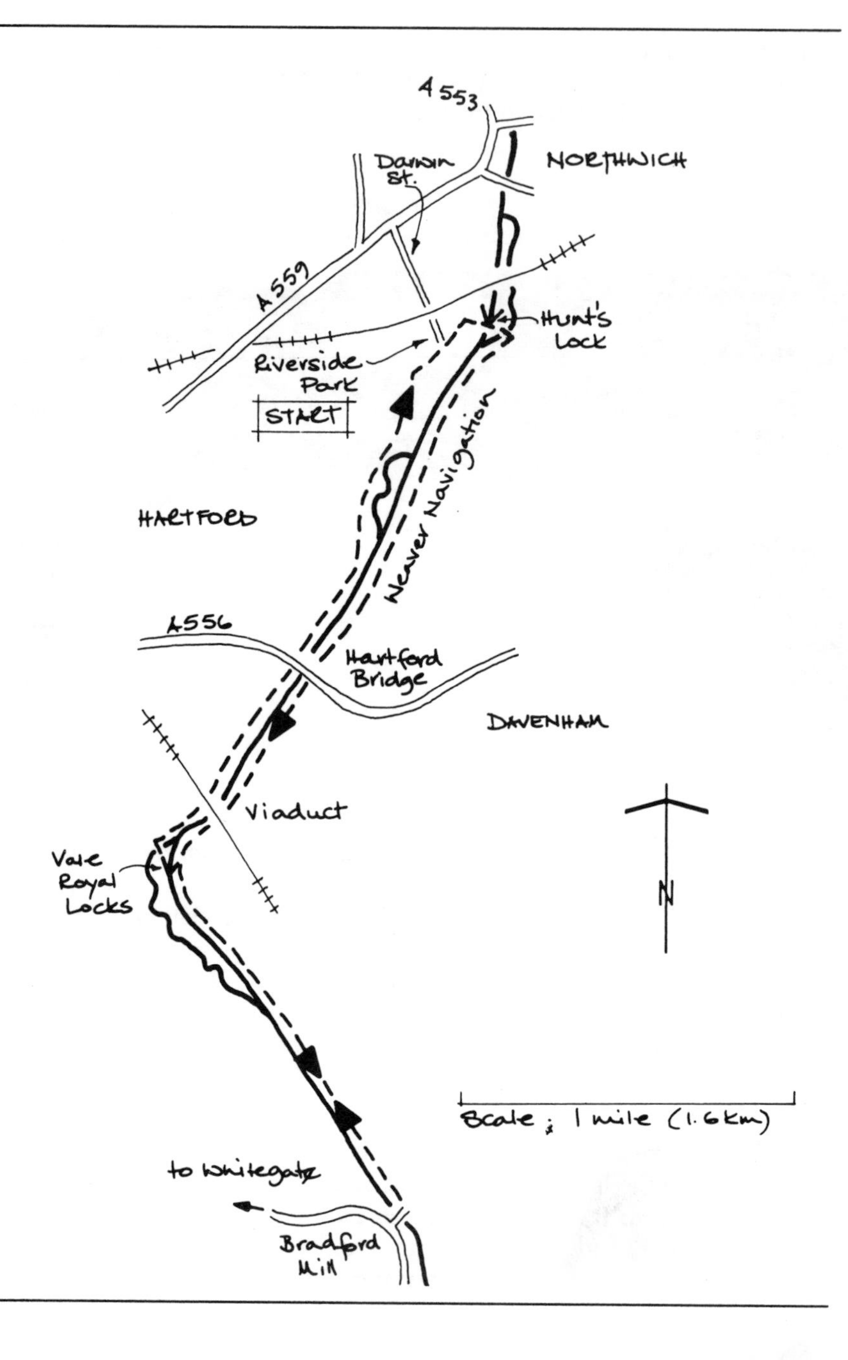
A 553
NORTHWICH
Darwin St.
A 559
Hunt's Lock
Riverside Park
START
Weaver Navigation
HARTFORD
A556
Hartford Bridge
DAVENHAM
Viaduct
Vale Royal Locks
N
Scale ; 1 mile (1.6 km)
to Whitegate
Bradford Mill

railway line over the river. Hunt's Locks are in splendid condition, brightly painted in black and white. Cross the first lock by way of the nearer set of double gates, and the second by the further set. From this point, one gets an impression of how deep the locks are on the Weaver. On the opposite bank, a path leads directly away from the lock. Follow it to a wooden footbridge over the channel parallel to the lock, leading to the weir. The footbridge, one of several along the Weaver, is a delightful structure, and is in fact a swingbridge. It is a trifle alarming to feel how much it bounces up and down!

Once over the bridge,turn right (if you want to have a look at the weir first, follow it to the left) and follow the weir channel until it rejoins the main line of the navigation again. This stretch of towpath runs alongside the backs of houses and gardens - but not for long. After a few hundred yards, one is in open country. This section of the river, with moorings and boat yards, always seems busy. Large barges and freighters tend to lurk beneath the viaduct at the foot of Hunt's Locks, while the stretch above bustles with all manner of smaller craft.

Old loops of the river branch off from the opposite bank. After about a mile, the path goes under the pale blue arches of Hartford Bridge. Close to the bridge was Hartford Lock, removed in Edward Leader Williams's improvements to the navigation in the late 19th century. There is no sign of the old lock, but the raised path along this section may indicate that the water level is not as high as when the lock existed. Even now, it would be difficult to get a very large vessel under Hartford Bridge, but it will take craft with 30 ft headroom. The new bridge was the last significant refinement to the Weaver. Prior to its construction in 1938, larger craft could not navigate as far as Winsford, due to the old stone bridge at Hartford. For years, there had been proposals for replacing it with a higher bridge, but the cost of building the Anderton Lift and four electrical powered swing bridges left the navigation's trustees little choice but to wait until the coffers were not quite so low.

In the meadow that follows, there are often horses roaming about - from my experience, they tend to be friendly, but not too curious. Trees line a steepish bank to the left, but the damp reedy land in between is clearly an old section of the river, doggedly refusing to be reclaimed.

Along the towpath, there are heavy iron chains and loops. They date back to when the navigation was in its heyday, and craft often had to queue up before going through the locks. Although it is only a short distance to Vale Royal Locks, little traffic uses it these days, and it is mainly pleasure craft that bothers to go upstream beyond Northwich.

Straight ahead are the impressive stone arches of the viaduct carrying the main west coast line over the Weaver. In fact, the same line crosses the Weaver again, some miles further north at Dutton. The sides of the navigation are thickly wooded here, and after the bridge it bends tightly to the left. Suddenly, Vale Royal Locks emerge. The path is wider and follows a slight incline to the locks.

Vale Royal Locks are quite superb. With their massive sandstone walls, and cast iron bridges, they are as fine as any locks in the north west. Beside the locks on the left are a row of cottages, and there are two swing bridges for pedestrians to cross the lock chambers. In crossing over, one can see the straight lines of Vale Royal Cut taking the navigation up to Winsford. Vale Royal Locks are the last locks on the navigation and, although craft can then follow the Weaver as far as Winsford Flashes, this has become a very quiet stretch.

Cross the locks by the two swing bridges, and then make your way over a sluice channel by a smaller bridge. The sluice gate controls the level of the upper section, and can be raised and lowered as appropriate. Follow the path to the right, down a slight slope to the old weir channel. With rivers in particular, it is necessary to have a weir parallel to locks to maintain the flow. The weir channel, here, which stretches for about half a mile is weedy and redundant, since the sluice gate has taken its place - providing a greater degree of control than a weir.

There is a bridge over the weir channel and, on the other side, there is an old land-locked loop of the Weaver. Follow the path between the two, turning right after the bridge. The path is well-defined, and a fence runs along one side. Beyond the old loop is the dense woodland of Vale Royal. The Weaver turns almost ninety degrees to the right, and the path follows it under the railway viaduct. Beyond this point, the path goes through a wooded glade for a hundred yards or so, before leading to a large blue and yellow sign with 'Weaver Navigation' on it.

The path becomes rather narrow and, this stretch being a favourite haunt of anglers, dips suddenly down to the water's edge in several places. The land to the left is steeply banked - here, the old course of the river ran exclusively off the opposite bank. It is a short distance to

Hartford Bridge, carrying the A556 Manchester to Chester Road. Go under the bridge, cross a stile, and follow a broad path on a slight embankment raised above the river on your right, and a wide expanse of pasture on your left.

After about three quarters of a mile, you come to part of the Weaver's old course, looping off to the left. This old stretch is full of weeds, and provides a home for the many types of ducks and wading birds that frequent these upper stretches of the Weaver. The navigation not only formed a deep channel for larger craft to make their way further up the Weaver, it got rid of tight bends which all too often held dangerous sandbanks. The path follows the old course, and crosses a stream that comes downhill from Hartford. Between the navigation and the old course, there is what almost is an island of land, which is the ideal setting for the boatyard there.

The path winds round to the left, and comes out at a tarmac track. Turn left and very shortly after, turn right. Follow this path for about fifty yards, then take it straight ahead through a small but thickly wooded area. The path leads back to the steps up to the Riverside Park and the start of the walk.

Canal Notes:

By 1721, an act had been passed, allowing the Weaver to be made navigable as far as Winsford. It was not until 1732, however, that vessels carrying as much as 45 tons were recorded as far as Northwich. Eleven locks were built and, over the the next twenty years, trade on the waterway more than doubled. After Northwich Lock collapsed in 1758, as a result of a rock salt pit caving in, substantial re-building began, and over the next fifty years, the original timber locks were replaced with brick and stone ones.

The Weaver remained prosperous into the 19th century, and a programme of improvements began in the late 1840s. This involved the creation of double locks to allow much larger vessels up the river, while the smaller ones ensured that water was not wasted when smaller craft passed through. The effects of the salt industry, however, led to further problems of subsidence, and the decision was finally taken in 1859 to do away with Northwich Lock. In 1865, the great canal builder, Edward Leader Williams, recommended that the number of locks on the navigation could be reduced to five, and this would clearly speed up traffic. Work began in 1871, and over £200,000 was spent on upgrading the Weaver over the next twenty years. When finished, it cut nearly two hours off the journey from Northwich to Weston Docks. By the turn of the century, however, the Weaver was carrying less and less salt and coal, although there was an expansion in the chemicals trade. With the building of a salt works at Weston Point, fed by pipes, trade on the Weaver was dealt a major blow. Yet, following the development of ICI, at Northwich, the Weaver came to be regarded as a valuable asset by the chemical industry.

To the walker, none of this sounds very appetising. Talk of chemicals inevitably leads to thoughts of pollution, of over-large tankers spilling inflammable or highly toxic cargoes into the river. It is a delightful surprise, then, to find the Weaver to be reasonably clear, and for there to be plenty of long sections unbesmirched by industry. The Weaver is a substantial river, and it is interesting to note how much it has resisted man's best efforts in taming it. Old loops and backwaters abound, and drained sections remain as marshland, refusing to dry out completely.

WALK 15: MOORE

Waterway: Runcorn and Latchford Canal

Distance: 5 miles

Start: Lapwing Lane crossroads, Moore, just across the Manchester Ship Canal from the village. Map reference: 578/854

Map: OS Pathfinder 739

How to get there: From Warrington, head towards Chester on the A5060, then A56. Turn right in to the A558, and it is about a mile to the right turn into Moore Lane which crosses Lapwing Lane. By bus from Warrington, take the 62, or 63 Moore service to the junction with Moore Lane.

This walk forms a figure of eight, and is about five miles long. It is not strenuous, but be prepared to fight through the more overgrown sections. Although the title of this book may imply that biblical powers are more important than strong shoes and weatherproof clothing, all of the walks are alongside canals, and not actually in them. All, that is, except this one. By now long disused, there is little to suggest that the Runcorn and Latchford Canal ever existed, and a large part of the walk that follows takes place along the canal bed.

Follow Chester Road (A5060, then A56) from Warrington, heading south west towards Chester. About a mile after the swing bridge over the Manchester Ship Canal, the road crosses the Bridgewater Canal. Just before this bridge, turn right in Runcorn Road (A558). After about a mile, turn right again, into Moore Lane. The road crosses a railway, and runs for almost half a mile before one comes across Moore Lane Swing Bridge, which crosses the Manchester Ship Canal. On the other side, a few yards straight ahead, there are crossroads. Start the walk from here.

The Walk:

Take the track straight ahead (Lapwing Lane). To the left is Lapwing Lane Wildfowl Reservoir - an odd shaped stretch of water that attracts

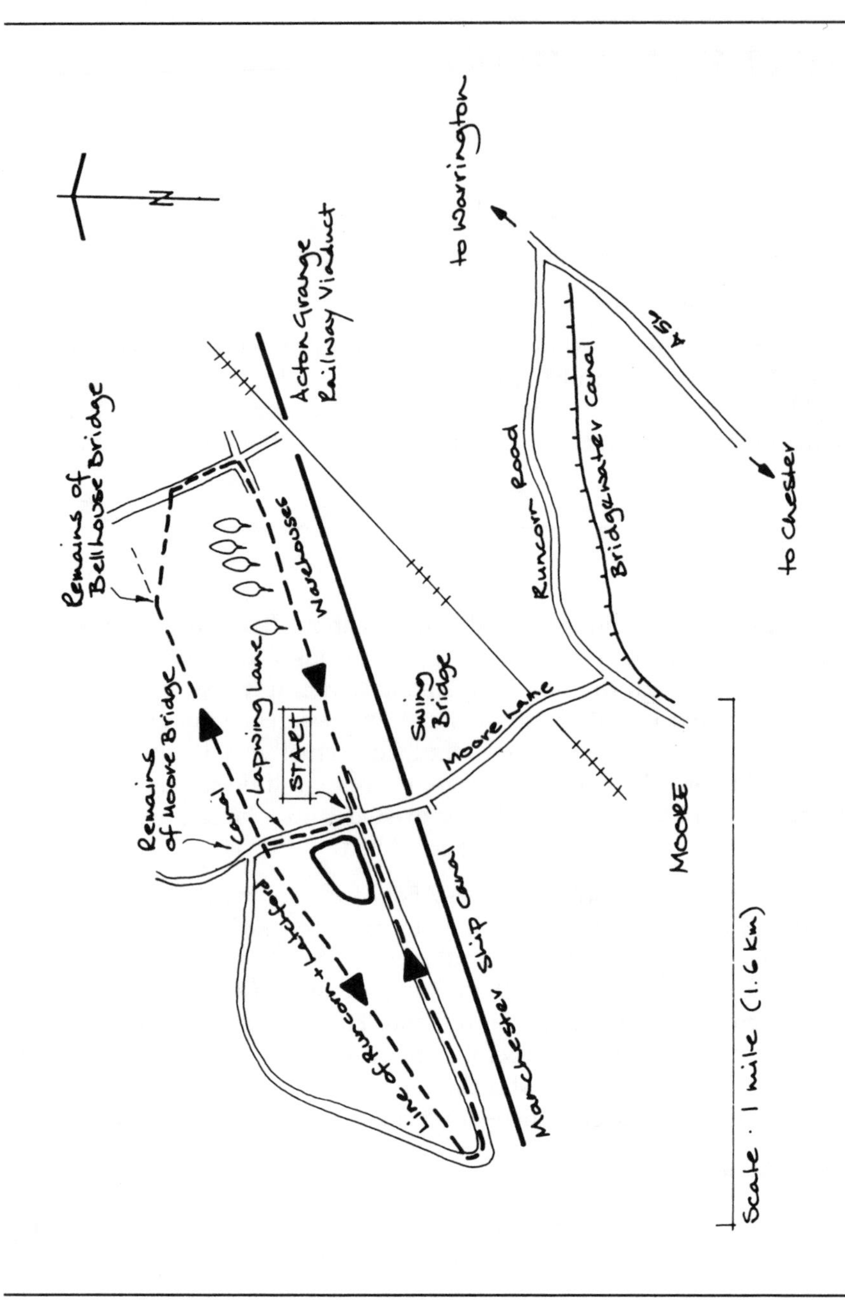
N
Remains of Bellhouse Bridge
Acton Grange Railway Viaduct
to Warrington
A56
to Chester
Runcorn Road
Bridgewater Canal
Warehouses
Lapwing Lane
START
Swing Bridge
Moore Lane
Remains of Moore Bridge
Canal
Line of Runcorn + Latchford Canal
Manchester Ship Canal
MOORE
Scale: 1 mile (1.6 Km)

ducks and wildfowl. Sticking up in the middle of the reservoir are dead trees, and one side is bounded by a steep bank of earth from the building of the Manchester Ship Canal. The sides of the track are densely wooded and, after about a quarter of a mile, there is a slight lump, which is all that remains of Moore Bridge. From the top, it is possible to see lines of trees stretching out on both sides, making the line of the canal, but it is difficult now to imagine how the Runcorn and Latchford Canal must have looked. On the other side, there are paths going off in both directions along what would have been the towpath.

Take the left-hand path. It becomes progressively narrower, beneath over-hanging trees. After a few hundred yards, the path drops down to the left, by way of a stone step - probably part of the canal bank. Follow the path down, and one is actually where the canal once was. The path is hard to follow from this point, but it is sufficient to ensure that one keeps between the canal banks. On the left is a steeper bank, and the reservoir is on the other side. As the canal gradually opens out, one can see the V-section of the canal bed, and small areas of the clay bottom still remain exposed.

A row of telegraph poles appear on the right, and their lines cross the canal. About eighty yards later, the canal is crossed by a track. The bridge has disappeared and one comes up against a steep bank. By crashing through the undergrowth for a few yards, it is possible to get onto the track on the left-hand side of the canal.

On the way up, there are great baulks of timber set deep in the earth, clearly relics of the old waterway. Follow the curving track left of the canal, up a slight incline. This provides a superb vantage point to view the mixture of industry and countryside south of Warrington. On the right is the sandstone Norton Water Tower, and the modern towers of Daresbury Scientific Research Centre, while the opposite side is dominated by the massif of Fiddler's Ferry Power Station. The track leads back to the crossroads.

Follow the track up to Moore Bridge again, and this time, turn right. Cross over a stile, and walk along a path lined with weeping willows and bullrushes for about three quarters of a mile. The path comes to a halt, and drops down to the left, beside a wooden post. There is a sandy track that forks, the left going over the remains of Bellhouse Bridge. Take the right fork, and follow it as it winds alongside a bank with a fence running along the top. Another path joins from the right, but keep to the path which follows the line of the fence. On the right hand side is Birch Wood.

After a few hundred yards, the large railway viaduct at Acton Grange emerges, taking the main west coast line over the Manchester Ship Canal. On the left, there is a flat expanse of earthworks. The path comes to a junction, turn right towards the viaduct. In the distance is the stonework of Twelve Arches, the viaduct carrying the railway over the River Mersey. About fifty yards later, turn right by a small building marked 'Laporte Bore Hole Number 5'. On one side of the track, there is a wire fence and warehouses, while the trees of Birch Wood are close at hand on the land dropping away to the right. Continue along the stony track, and return to the crossroads.

Canal Notes:

The Runcorn and Latchford Canal (also known as the Old Quay Canal) was built as a short cut from the Mersey estuary at Runcorn to Warrington, missing out the worst of the river's meanderings. In 1796, the Old Quay Company (the owners of the Mersey and Irwell Navigation) began to consider an improvement fo the route between Warrington and Runcorn, with a view to enhancing trade between Manchester and Liverpool. It was agreed to by-pass the river with a canal on its south side, and work began in 1799. The cut was completed in 1804, and ran from Manor Lock (formerly Latchford Lock), south of Warrington, to the Old Quay, Runcorn, just north of where its direct competitor, the Bridgewater Canal, also joined the Mersey estuary.

The canal was widely used by 'Mersey Flats' - barges about 66 ft long by 15 ft and built of timber. These boats were gaff-rigged, with a large mainsail and small foresail. Before proper towpaths were built, the flats were pulled by teams of men, if there was insufficient wind. With the advent of of towpaths, horses took over. In order to navigate shallow stretches of the river, the Mersey Flats drew only about three feet of water, and could carry up to 35 tons of cargo.In the eighteenth century, trade along the 7 $^3/_4$ mile Runcorn and Latchford Canal expanded as both the Mersey and Irwell Navigation, of which it formed a part, and its rival, the Bridgewater Canal grew busier. The two waterways fought each other hard, offering traffic all manner of special rates. A wide variety of cargoes were carried on the canal, from sugar to pig-iron, and at the Runcorn end, the old docks handled chemicals, grain and timber. In fact, it has been said that cotton bales were piled up to 9 ft high on the decks of the Mersey Flats.

A difficulty that the canal faced was that it started at Latchford by rising from the Mersey, and ended at Runcorn by descending into it again. This meant that the canal was drained at both ends, and an artificial feeeder had to be built, taking water along a wooden trough from much further up the Mersey. When the Manchester Ship Canal was built, the Runcorn and Latchford Canal was rendered obsolete. In fact, it cut right through the old canal, part of which went to form a link between the Manchester Ship Canal and the River Mersey (this stretch from Manor Lock to the new junction with the Manchester Ship Canal at Twenty Steps Lock became known as the 'Black Bear Canal' after an old pub along the route), while the rest fell into disrepair. The Black Bear Canal has since been filled in and the only section of the Runcorn and Latchford Canal that remains is a small stretch, beside where Chester Road crosses an old loop of the River Mersey, south of Warrington.

WALK 16: WOOLSTON AND THELWALL

Waterways: River Mersey and Manchester Ship Canal

Distance: Under 5 miles

Start: Paddington Bank, Warrington, just off the A50. Map reference: 626/888

Map: OS Pathfinder 740

How to get there: From Warrington, take the A57 towards Manchester, turn right into the A50, and then a quarter of a mile further on turn left into Paddington Bank. By bus from Warrington, take the 10 Manchester service to the junction of the A50 and A57.

This walk, which is less than five miles long, could hardly be described as scenic, but it gives a fascinating glimpse into the evolution of the Mersey and Irwell Navigation, and how it was superseded by the construction of the Manchester Ship Canal. It follows the line of a disused canal, the River Mersey, and the Manchester Ship Canal itself. With each year, less and less remains of the old navigation.

Start the walk from Paddington Bank, just outside Warrington. Heading out of the town centre on the A57 Manchester Road, turn right at the traffic lights where there is the junction with the A50 Kingsway North. A quarter of a mile to the left is a road named Paddington Bank.

The Walk:

At the end of the short road, there is a gate on the right hand side, leading out to the River Mersey. Turn left on the path, part of the Mersey Valley Way, which follows the north bank of the river as it curves in a big loop round to the left.

Very soon after joining the path, it crosses the old entrance to the now abandoned Woolston New Cut. In the days of the old Mersey and Irwell Navigation, before the Manchester Ship Canal was built, it provided a

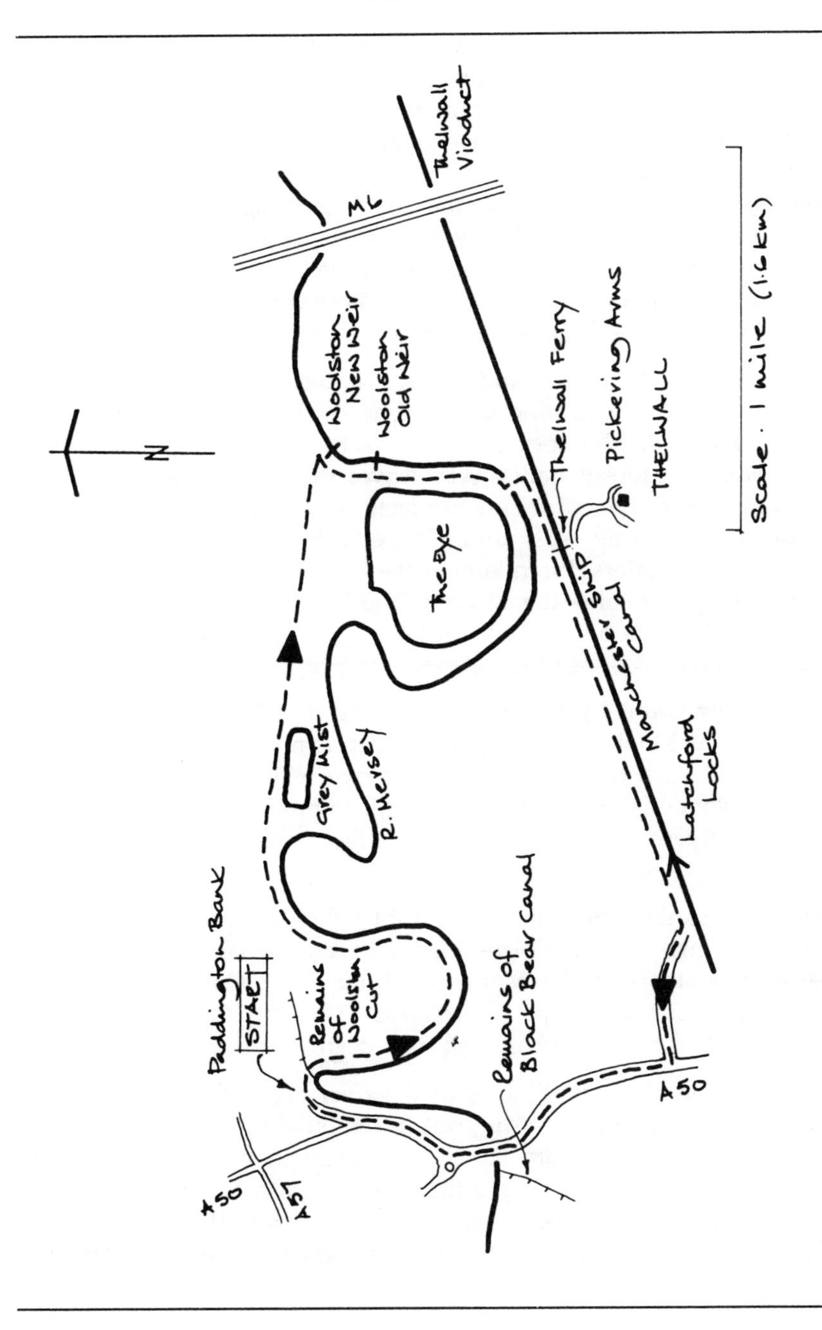
N
Thelwall Viaduct
M6
Woolston New Weir
Woolston Old Weir
Thelwall Ferry
Pickering Arms
THELWALL
Scale . 1 mile (1.6km)
The Eye
Manchester Ship Canal
Latchford Locks
Grey Mist
R. Mersey
Paddington Bank
START
Remains of Woolston Cut
Remains of Black Bear Canal
A50
A57
A50

valuable means of avoiding the dangerous and time-consuming loops of the Mersey along this stretch. Opened in 1821, the New Cut was two miles long, and came out upstream above Woolston Weir. Today, there is little to show that the cut ever existed, but there are some remains of the chamber of Paddington Lock. Almost opposite the lock, there used to be a wooden trough across the river, carrying water, taken from further upstream from the Mersey, to feed the nearby Black Bear Canal. The feeder was vital to the Mersey and Irwell Navigation as the Black Bear was higher than either of the two waterways it joined, and quickly lost level whenever a craft locked out of it.

Pass the entrance to the cut, and follow the river as it bends around first to the left, then starts turning to the right to circle the old farming land of Oatland Eye. At the apex of the bend, the river and the cut almost meet. Here, the Mersey Valley Way leaves the river bank, and instead follows the line of the cut. There are factories on the left of the cut, and the two ponds, Grey Mist and Cooper's Pit, which are invariably surrounded by anglers. From joining the line of the cut, it is just over a mile to where it rejoins the Mersey. The lock keeper's cottage is still there, but what was once Woolston Lock, joining the cut and the river, has since been turned into the cottage's garden!

The path comes out by the river. Spanning it is Woolston New Weir, with its unusual-looking sluice gates, which is now principally used for flood control. Turn right, and follow the river past Woolston Old Weir, a more conventional weir which was built to produce a more navigable channel upstream for craft locking into the river from Woolston Old Cut.

Dating back to the 1760s, the old cut, of which nothing at all remains today, was situated between the New Cut, and Woolston Old Weir. It bypassed one loop of the Mersey, but the New Cut replaced it by avoiding two further loops. From 1755, Thelwall Gunpowder Mills stood by the Old Weir, until an explosion destroyed them in the 1850s.

Beyond the Old Weir, both sides of the river are built up with 'eyes', flat-topped mounds of earth dug out in the building of the Manchester Ship Canal. Today, they are home for a great many species of birds. Less than half a mile after joining the river, the path crosses a footbridge over the Mersey. On the other side, it slopes downhill to the banks of the Manchester Ship Canal. To the left is the great curve of the Thelwall

Viaduct, carrying the M6 motorway across the river and the canal. Turn right, and follow the wide path alongside the canal. After about a quarter of a mile, the path passes the Thelwall Ferry.

For those with plenty of time, it is well worth the 10p trip across. In the days when the canal had more traffic, it could be an alarming experience to head slowly across the canal in a tiny, flat-bottomed boat, with ocean-going freighters drawing ever nearer! On the other side of the canal, it is only a short walk into pretty Thelwall village, and its delightful pub, The Pickering Arms.

Back to the walk. Follow the path, with the canal on the left. After about three quarters of a mile, the canal comes to Latchford Locks, the last ones on the Manchester Ship Canal before the sea locks at Eastham and the entrance to the Mersey estuary. Beyond the locks, follow Thelwall Lane, the road leading gradually away to the right. After passing through a housing estate, the road comes out at the A50 Kingsway South. Turn right, and follow the main road for half a mile to the bridge over the Mersey.

Just to the left of the bridge, the Black Bear Canal (the local name for the Latchford end of the Runcorn and Latchford Canal) used to join the Mersey by way of Manor Lock, built in 1804. There is little left of it today. This canal, which also formed part of the Mersey and Irwell Navigation, helped boats to miss out the downstream meanderings of the Mersey, with their sandbanks and shallows. Craft heading upstream towards Manchester would then join the Mersey at Manor Lock, head under the bridge, and leave the river again at Paddington Lock to follow Woolston New Cut up to Woolston Lock, where they would rejoin the river.

Under the bridge used to be the feeder running into the Black Bear Canal on the far side of Manor Lock. Cross the bridge, and it is less than half a mile to Paddington Bank, this time on the right hand side, and the start of the walk.

WALK 17: NORTON

Waterway: Bridgewater Canal Runcorn Branch

Distance: 6 miles

Start: Preston Brook. Map reference: 568/807

Map: OS Pathfinder 739

How to get there: From junction 11 of the M56, take the A56 towards Frodsham to where it crosses the canal. From Warrington, take the C30 or C31 Chester services.

This is not a strenuous walk, and is about six miles long. Some parts can get rather muddy, so strong shoes, or boots are recommended. Refreshments can be bought at Norton Priory Museum and, near to Preston Brook Bridge, there is the Red Lion, which sells Greenall Whitley's beers. The main attraction of this walk is to discover how successfully history, industry, housing and countryside have been integrated. Along some parts of the canal, it is possible to imagine being miles from the nearest house. While the canals, the two railway lines, and the motorway snake in and out of each other to form a dense network of transport systems, there is nevertheless a delightful feeling of seclusion.

Start the walk from Preston Brook, where the A56 crosses the Trent and Mersy Canal just south of its junction with the Bridgewater Canal. Preston Brook is very close by, and is signposted from junction 11 of the M56.

The Walk:

The towpath is on the west side of the canal. Take the tarmac track down to it heading north, in the direction of the M56 viaduct. The track runs alongside a row of pretty cottages and there is a marina on the opposite bank. Follow the track under the motorway, to where the Trent and Mersy ends, and the Bridgewater leads off north west to Runcorn, and north east to Manchester. The track winds to the left, alongside the

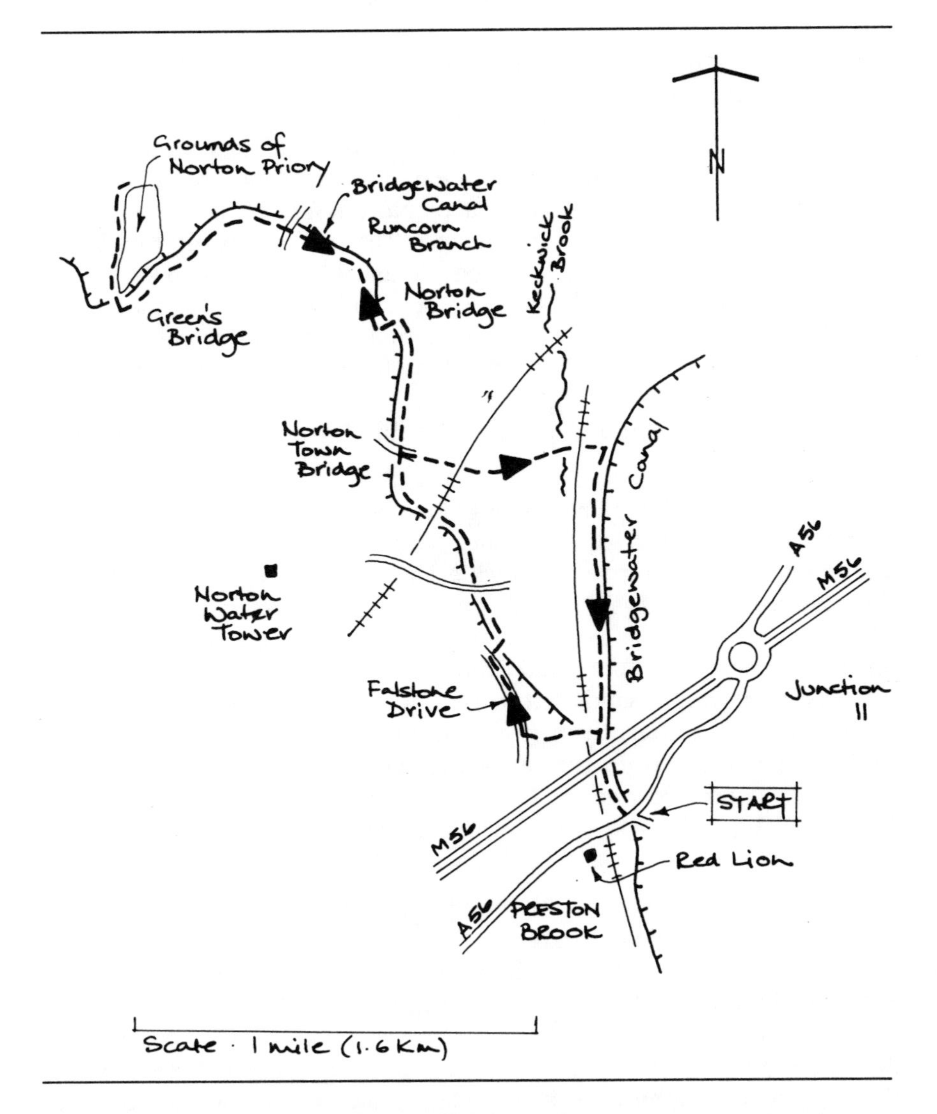

Runcorn branch. Although the Runcorn branch of the Canal now terminates at Waterloo Bridge, the Bridgewater Canal originally descended via a flight of ten, large, double locks to Runcorn Docks which led out to the Mersey estuary. The docks were also connected by the Runcorn and Weston canal to the River Weaver. After the construction of the Manchester Ship Canal, Runcorn Docks were used less and less. Finally, in 1966 the locks connecting them with the canal were filled in.

Cross over the main west coast railway, set in a deep cutting, and follow a path that bears to the left, away from the canal, heading in the direction of the sandstone rotunda of Norton Water Tower - one of North Cheshire's best known landmarks. The path comes up to a fence, and leads into a new estate, built beside an old inlet known as Duke's Wharf (after the Duke of Bridgewater). Follow the road that bears slightly to the left, and take the first right after the estate (Falstone Drive). It is a narrow road, running along the backs of houses. The road rises, and there is a turning to the right that crosses the canal. Turn right, cross the bridge and go down to the towpath on the left hand side.

Dead ahead are the giant cooling towers of Fiddler's Ferry power station, and the tower of Daresbury science research laboratory is on your right. It is not far to the brick arches of Borrow's Bridge (69). On the other side, there is a winch on the opposite bank to lower stop planks into the grooves beside the canal. This point is a long way from any locks, and a leak here could drain extremely long sections of several canals. The towpath winds left to go under the Warrington to Chester railway line. Just after, there is an overflow, roaring with the flow, to drain excess water from the canal into the brook below. To the right, there is a superb view across the flat expanse of the Mersey estuary as far as Winter Hill. The two concrete towers in the distance are the covered workings of Parkside Colliery near Newton le Willows.

The next bridge is Norton Town Bridge. The spire to the left is St Mary's, Halton, which stands on the brow of the hill close to the remains of Halton Castle. The church was designed by Sir Giles Gilbert Scott in 1851. After Norton Town Bridge comes Norton Bridge (72). Here the towpath changes sides. Although there has been a good deal of new building in Norton, the canal is relatively unspoilt, and passes through some delightful, leafy stretches. New Norton Bridge and Old Norton Bridge are close together, then the canal turns sharply to the left, and heads towards Green's Bridge (75).

Before the bridge, take the path up the left hand side, and cross over. Go through an iron gate and follow a well made path with playing fields to the left. After about half a mile, there is a black iron gate set in the fence running along the paths's right hand side. This leads to the entrance to Norton Priory Museum. Norton Priory was built to house twenty four Augustinian canons in 1134. Since then, it has been turned into a Tudor, then a Georgian mansion by the Brooke Family. In 1921, the building was abandoned. Today, there are sixteen acres of woodlands and gardens, the excavated remains of the priory, the 12th century undercroft, and the museum. In the grounds of Norton Priory, there are all manner of things to discover. There is an 18th century summerhouse, and a herb garden. In 1977, a replica of a medieval bell was cast, after a 13th century bell mould was discovered during excavations, and is situated in the gardens. There is even a medieval sandstone coffin to be found.

From the museum, take the path back to Green's Bridge, and follow the towpath back towards Preston Brook. Just after Norton Town Bridge (71), with the railway ahead, there is a stone step leading off to the left. Climb over, and take the cinder path downhill to the right. It is a curious mixture of urban and rural. Despite the presence of so much industry, this area has remained wholly unspoilt. The path crosses a small brook,and leads to an arch under the Warrington to Chester railway. On the other side, the line of the path peters out, but the line is marked by a telegraph pole in the middle of the field, and the wooden bridge beyond.

The bridge crosses Keckwick Brook and on the other side, a yellow arrow points to the left. Follow the path left, to another arrow pointing right. The path goes down to a rickety looking bridge over a stream. On the other side, there is a path leading to an arch under the west coast railway line. It is very low and, on the other side, there is a steep scramble up a muddy bank and into a field. Cross the field.

Although there is no apparent path, aim for the set of steps dead ahead on the other side of the field. Go up the steps, and there is the Bridgewater Canal. Turn right onto the towpath. The canal is quite broad here, and follows a contour line, being set into the side of the land rising up to Preston on the Hill. After a few hundred yards, the canal crosses the pretty Red Brow, leading steeply up to Daresbury. It is not far to the junction with the Trent and Mersey Canal. Cross the footbridge, over the entrance to the Runcorn branch of the Bridgewater Canal, and head under the motorway viaduct back to Preston Brook.

A narrowboat heading towards Norton

WALK 18: DARESBURY TO WALTON GARDENS

Waterway: Bridgewater Canal

Distance: 5 miles

Start: Daresbury church. Map reference: 580/829

Map: OS Pathfinder 739

How to get there: From Warrington, head towards Chester on the A56 to Daresbury, the village being just to the left of the main road. By bus from Warrington, take the C30, or C31 Chester services.

This is a gentle walk of about five miles, and follows well-marked paths. The grounds of Walton Hall are particularly attractive and well worth a diversion. I find this section of countryside around the Bridgewater Canal particularly remarkable as it is so pretty and unspoilt, yet in close proximity to one of the largest groupings of heavy industy in Britain. Incidentally, Daresbury's first syllable is pronounced 'dar' not 'dare'.

The Walk:

Start the walk from Daresbury Church. All Saints, Daresbury has a perpendicular tower, but the rest of the church is 19th century. Charles Lutwidge Dodgson (Lewis Carroll) was born at Daresbury in 1832, and his father was vicar of Daresbury. Heading north from junction 11 on the M56, it is about a mile and a half along the A56, on the right. From the junction beside the church, walk across to the Ring O' Bells pub, which serves Greenall's beer. Facing the pub, turn left, and follow the road out of the village for a quarter of a mile. To the right, there is a footpath sign, leading off by a small shop. Follow the footpath the short distance to the set of steps leading down to the A56. Cross the road, and ascend the steps on the opposite side.

The path is not very clear, but it winds to the left, following the edge of a field. It drops downhill, and provides a good view of Runcorn bridge across where the Mersey narrows. Runcorn road bridge was built in the

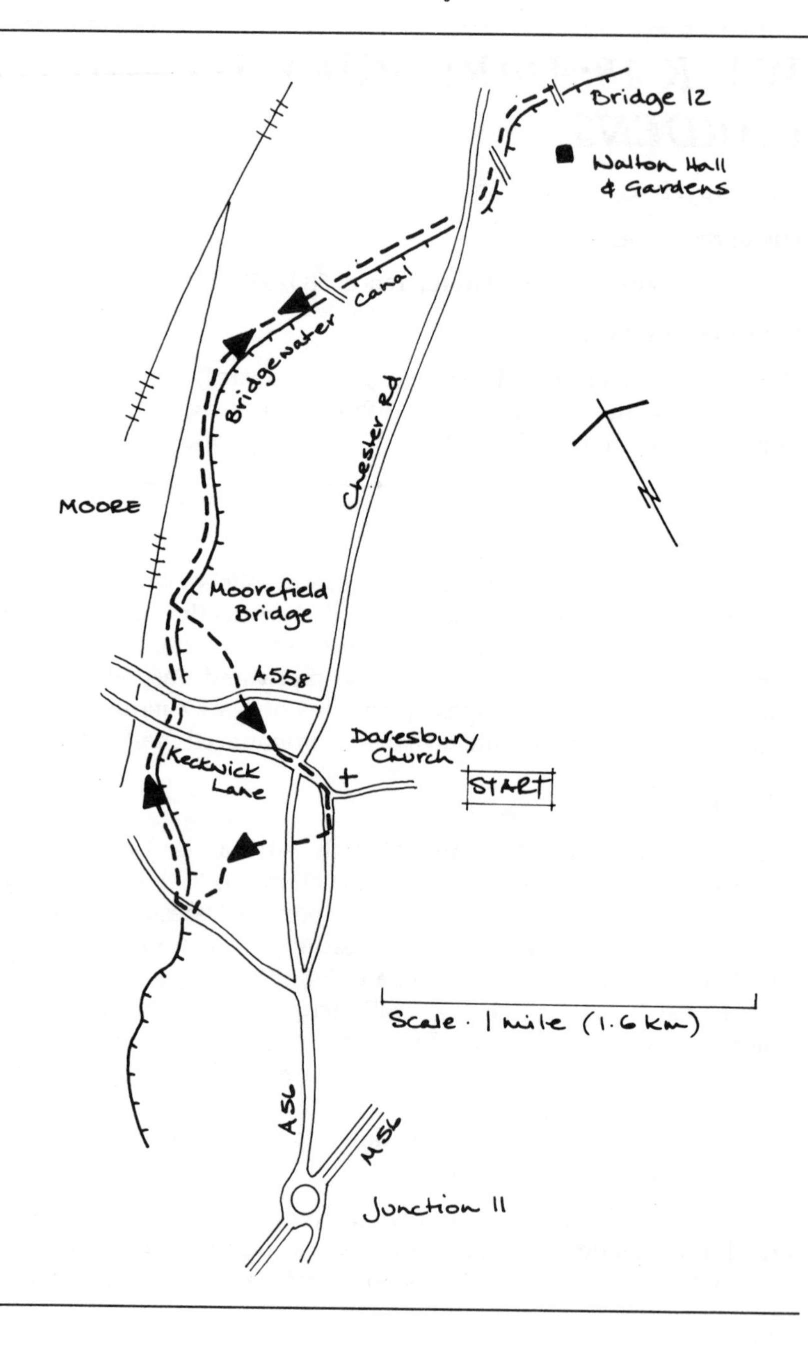
Bridge 12
Walton Hall
& Gardens
Canal
Bridgewater
Chester Rd
N
MOORE
Moorefield
Bridge
A558
Daresbury
Church
START
Keckwick
Lane
Scale · 1 mile (1.6 km)
A56
M56
Junction 11

late 1950s. It is particularly elegant, being a single arch with a span of over 1000 feet. When it was built, it was the largest steel arch in Europe, and the third largest in the world. The road bridge replaced a transporter bridge built at the turn of the century.

The path comes out on a road about fifty yards from the Bridgewater Canal. Turn right, and cross the bridge to the towpath. Once on the towpath, head off to the right. It is not far from George Gleaves's bridge to Keckwick Hill bridge. From here, the canal runs close to the Warrington to Chester railway line, which keeps its straight line by going through tunnels, cuttings,and over embankments. The tall white tower on the right hand side is part of the science research laboratory, which specialises in nuclear research. The canal passes under Keckwick Bridge (5), a modern road bridge, and Moorefield Bridge before running along the eastern edge of Moore, a pretty village set in the small strip of rural land between Warrington and Runcorn. At Moorefield Bridge, there is a crane to lower stop planks into the canal. From Moore Bridge (7), the village is only a hundred yards away, and refreshments can be obtained from the attractive Red Lion Hotel. After Moore, the canal begins to wind round to the right, to head in a more easterly direction. It passes under Acton Grange Bridge and Thomason's Bridge before coming to the curious concrete arches of Chester road bridge, carrying the A56 across. It is a very short distance from this busy road to the leafy seclusion of Higher Walton.

After Walton Bridge (11), the canal is thickly wooded to Walton Lea Bridge (12) and beyond. Once under bridge 12, take the set of steps up to the road, and cross over the bridge. This leads directly into the grounds of Walton Hall, with its splendid conservatory, rose arbours, and even a small zoo. Walton Hall was the home of Sir Gilbert Greenall (founder of Greenall Whitley, the Warrington brewery). It was built in the 1830s, with the additions in 1870. From Walton Hall, the best way back is to follow the towpath along the canal back as far as Moore.

By Moorefield Bridge, take the path up the side of the bridge and cross over. On the other side, the path bears right, and leads steadily uphill to come out at a footpath sign on the A558 expressway. Cross over, and follow the path uphill the short distance to Keckwick Lane. A set of steps goes down to the road. Turn left, and follow the narrow lane up to the A56 Chester Road. Cross the road, and it is a couple of hundred yards along the lane back to Daresbury Church.

WALK 19: GRAPPENHALL

Waterway: Bridgewater Canal

Distance: Just under 8 miles

Start: Grappenhall village. Map reference: 640/863

Map: OS Pathfinder 740

How to get there: From Warrington, take the A50 towards Knutsford, shortly after the junction with the A56, the left turn to Grappenhall is well signposted. By bus from Warrington, take the 47 Knutsford service.

The walk is just under eight miles long. Although only half of the walk follows the canal, the return journey provides panoramic views that help to put the Bridgewater Canal into the context of the Mersey Valley landscape.

Start the walk from Grappenhall village, which is best approached by taking the A50 Knutsford Road, from Junction 20 of the M6 motorway, towards Warrington. The road crosses the Bridgewater Canal, shortly after turning left into Bellhouse Lane. After about a quarter of a mile, the road comes up to bridge 17, and the attractive village of Grappenhall with its cobbled street and stocks. There are also two attractive pubs, 'The Ram's Head' and 'Parr Arms', where refreshments may be bought.

The Walk:

Take the slope down the right hand side of the bridge down to the towpath on the opposite side of the canal from St Wilfrid's Church, Grappenhall. Follow the towpath away from the bridge. For the next quarter of a mile, the canal curves to your left, and goes under Stanny Lunt bridge (16). While the canal winds alongside the A56 Chester Road on the opposide bank, the ground rises to the south. After about a mile, the canal crosses Lumb Brook by a squat, heavy aqueduct. The brook rises to the south, near Appleton Thorn, and drains into the Manchester Ship Canal. From the aqueduct, one can survey the industrial landscape

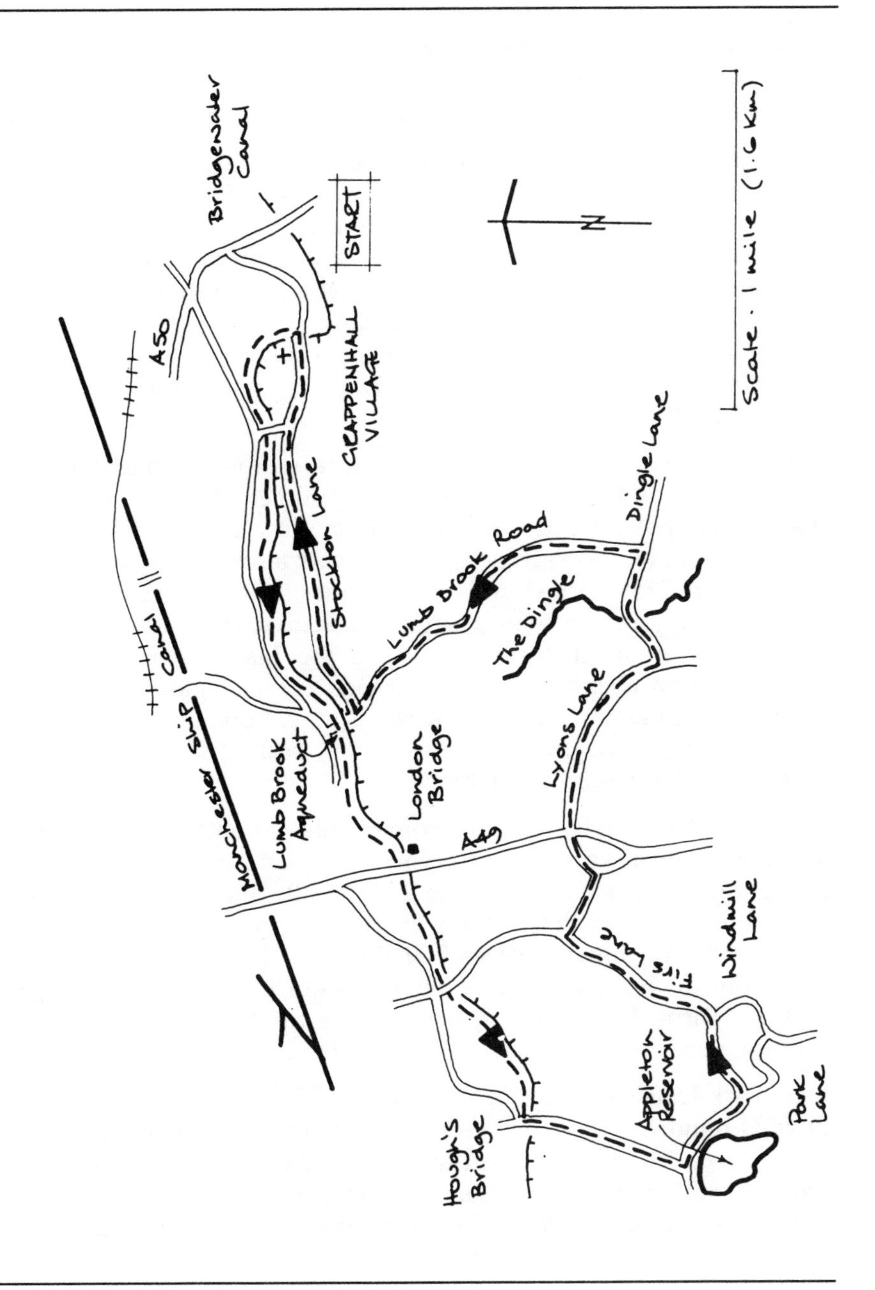
Bridgewater Canal
START
N
Scale · 1 mile (1.6 Km)
A50
GRAPPENHALL VILLAGE
Stockton Lane
Lumb Brook Road
Dingle Lane
The Dingle
Manchester Ship Canal
Lumb Brook Aqueduct
London Bridge
Lyons Lane
A49
Windmill Lane
Firs Lane
Appleton Reservoir
Park Lane
Hough's Bridge

of Warrington on the right hand side. To the west, there are the cooling towers of Fiddler's Ferry Power Station, in the distance is the smooth arc of Winter Hill with its radio masts, and the west is marked by the splendid steeple of St Elphin's, Warrington, one of the highest in Britain.

The next half mile stretch is busy with pleasure craft, as there are moorings and an inlet on the opposite bank just before the A49 London Road Bridge. Beside the bridge, there is a flight of stone steps by the canal. They date back to the end of the 18th century, when a service of passenger boats ran between Stockton Heath, to the south of Warrington, and Manchester. Although converted barges were first used for this service, in 1774 two packet boats were specially built for the Duke of Bridgewater. On these, there were first, second and third class cabins, and a coffee room.

On the other side of the bridge, there is a small cafe, and the canal curves its way on to Red Lane Bridge. Beyond here, heavy trees line the canal. This densely wooded section is home to a great many different species of bird. Not a great many people walk along this towpath, here, so be prepared for startled birds to dart out of the trees as one follows the canal. The canal crosses a small brook that is an overflow from Appleton Reservoir that runs down to the Manchester Ship Canal opposite Walton Lock and the old entrance to Warrington Dock. About a mile after Red Lane Bridge is Hough's Bridge. Leave the towpath, and cross the bridge. Hough's Lane rises gently, past Beechtree Farm, with Walton Hall Gardens on the right.

After about half a mile, the lane comes out at Appleton Reservoir. A high concrete wall keeps the reservoir at bay and one can walk along the top of it. Turn left, and follow the wall. From here, there is a splendid view of the interlocking canals, rivers and railways to the south of Warrington. At the end of the wall, Park Lane leads away uphill from the reservoir. Follow the lane until it becomes a track, past Daintith's Farm. From the top, one can see right across the wide flat land formed by the River Mersey on its way to the sea.

Where Park Lane comes out at a junction, turn left up Firs Lane. After a couple of hundred yards, the track winds its way further up Hill Cliffe, along a deep, dripping gorge cut through sandstone. Even in the hottest weather, overhanging trees keep out the sun, and the red walls on either side are always running with water. Follow Firs Lane into suburbia. Fortunately, this disappears again within half a mile. Turn right into Windmill Lane, left into Quarry Lane, cross London Road, and follow Lyons Lane as it winds around to your right. After passing Longwood Road, turn left into Dingle Lane. This dips down to 'The Dingle', a wooded dell crossing Dodd's Brook.

A quarter of a mile further on, the lane climbs uphill to Lumb Brook Road. Turn left, and follow the road for a mile down to the Bridgewater Canal's Lumb Brook Aqueduct. Just before the canal, Stockton Lane leads up, on the right hand side. Passing Mountain Farm, on the right, Stockton Lane comes out alongside the canal. For the next mile, the lane runs beside the canal, for short stretches right against it. The lane comes out at Stanny Lunt Bridge. Turn right into Church Lane, and follow it through Grappenhall village, past the church and the set of stocks that remain outside it, to Grappenhall Bridge.

Canal Notes:

There has been a good deal of debate over the years as to which is the country's oldest canal. Whatever case is made, however, the Bridgewater Canal was the first canal to be built in England as a commercial waterway, and one which does not simply follow the line of a river. The Bridgewater Canal was built essentially to cary coal from the 3rd Duke of Bridgewater's mines in Worsley and Walkden. Without the genius of James Brindley, however, the canal could never have been built. It was Brindley who overcame the many technical difficulties that the waterway faced. When such a problem arose, Brindley would take to his bed for a period of days at a time, and finally get up when he had the solution. Brindley died in 1772, before the canal was finished. Only 56 years old, during the last 13 years of his life, Brindley engineered over 350 mile of canals.

Despite the fact that in 1762, the Duke of Bridgewater had received permission to extend his canal as far as the Mersey estuary at Runcorn, the completion of the Bridgewater canal involved a good deal of negotiations and expense. The competition offered by the Mersey and Irwell Navigation, and construction of the Trent and Mersey Canal had a profound effect on the Dukes's plans.

By 1770, the canal had worked its way westward as far as Lumb Brook, and reached London Road Bridge at Stockton Heath in 1771. At this stage, goods bound for Liverpool were transferred from the canal to the River Mersey at Warrington. It remained the western terminus until the completion of the canal in 1776. The successsful growth of the passenger service on the canal led to two boats operating between Runcorn and Manchester. Stockton Heath, nevertheless, remained an important interchange, and passengers could disembark there to catch a coach into Liverpool. The passenger boats were 56 ft long, and 8ft wide, and journeys from Runcorn to Manchester took eight hours with stops to change horses.

Following the Manchester Ship Canal's completion, one might have imagined that trade on the Bridgewater canal would be severely reduced, as the two waterways run parallel. While some trade was lost, the Bridgewater Canal also benefited from the vast amount of trade the ship canal brought up to Manchester, as it was used to transport smaller cargoes to points out of Manchester. By World War One, almost 2 million tons per year were carried on the Bridgewater Canal. With the growth of the road network, however, trade gradually wound down, and today very little commercial traffic is seen on the canal.

WALK 20: LYMM

Waterways: Bridgewater Canal, Manchester Ship Canal

Distance: Just under 4 miles

Start: The Spread Eagle, Lymm. Map reference: 681/873

Map: OS Pathfinder 740

How to get there: From junction 7 on the M56, it is five miles to Lymm along the A56, and the right turn in to the centre of the village. By bus from Warrington, take the 37 Altrincham service.

Lymm is one of Cheshire's prettiest villages, on a interesting site which is riddled with streams, pools and canals. This is a short walk, just under four miles long, but one which can be extended.

The Walk:

Start the walk from The Spread Eagle, a pub which sells Lees beers. To get to Lymm, head along the A56 from junction 7 of the M56 towards Warrington. After about five miles, there is a right turn into Lymm village, along Eagle Brow. The pub is a few hundred yards down the hill, on the right hand side of the road. Just beyond the pub, there is an estate agents on a corner. Turn right into the path that runs alongside it and The Dingle, a stream leading down to the Manchester Ship Canal that forms a pool beside Eagle Brow, where a steep clough takes the water down under the road.

The stream narrows, and the path runs through thick woodland for about a quarter of a mile. A set of steps leads up to Church Road, the A56. Cross over the road and, immediately opposite is the large, man-made pool known as Lymm Dam. Take the path that runs along the right hand side of the dam. Formed by the confluence of Mag Brook and Bradley Brook, the dam ensures a controlled flow of water down the steep and narrow ravine of The Dingle.

The path follows the edge of the dam, and small bridges cross over the streams that feed it. Follow the path round, back towards St Mary's

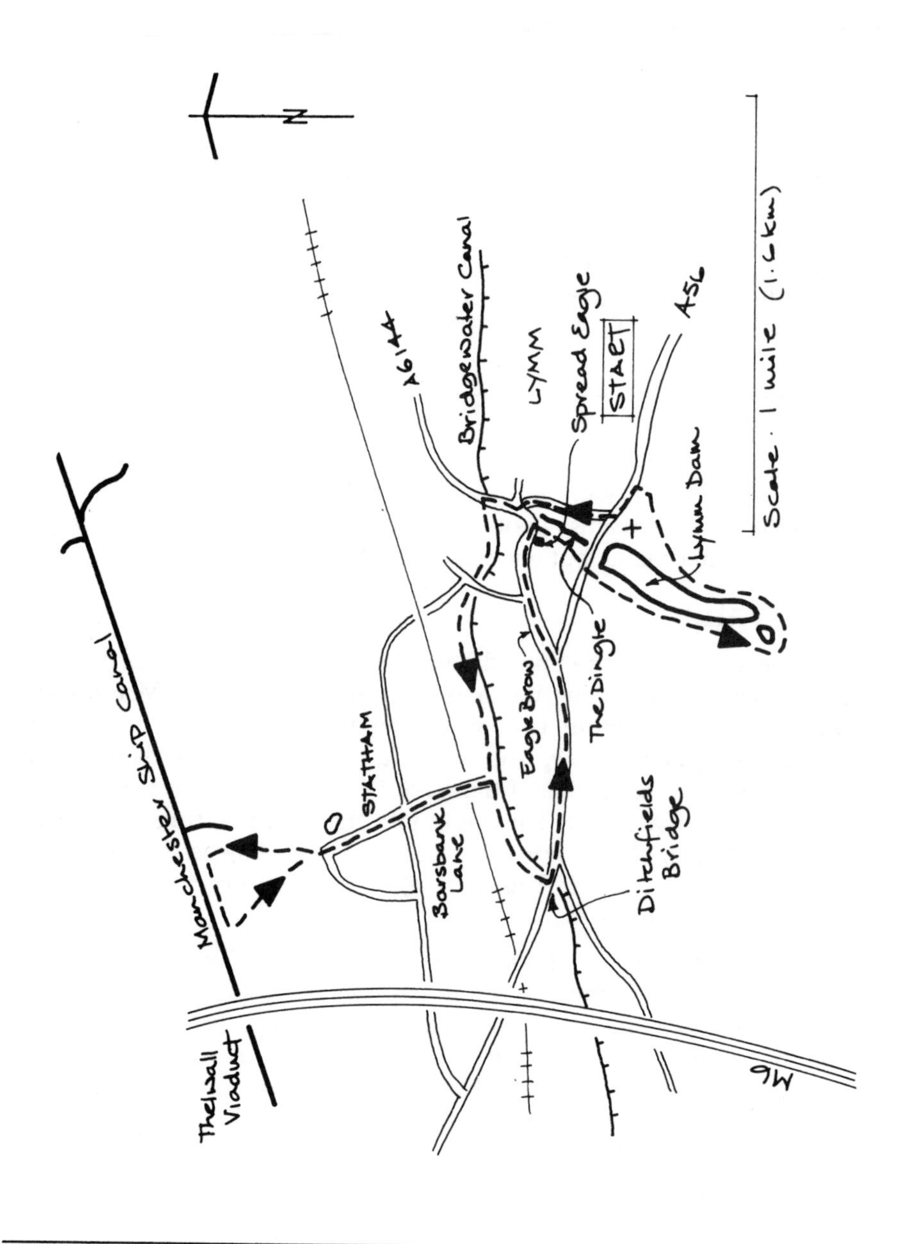
N
Manchester Ship Canal
Thelwall Viaduct
STATHAM
Barsbank Lake
Eagle Brow
The Dingle
Ditchfields Bridge
A6144
Bridgewater Canal
LYMM
Spread Eagle
START
A56
Lymm Dam
M6
Scale: 1 mile (1.6km)

church, with its tall, square tower. Back at the main road, cross over and turn right. A little way along is Rectory Lane. Follow the steep road downhill to the 17th century cross in the centre of Lymm. At the cross, turn right, and follow the road past two pubs, and over the bridge across the Bridgewater Canal. On the far side, the towpath can be joined on the right hand side. Head back under the bridge, and follow the towpath along the canal. Winding through the village on a higher level, it is not far to the aqueduct where the canal crosses The Dingle. This is invariably a busy stretch, and a popular mooring. Shortly after, the canal is shaded by large trees, and almost appears to be in a cutting.

Where the canal crosses Barsbank Lane, it is possible to extend the walk with a visit to the old course of the River Mersey. Leave the Bridgewater Canal, and head downhill along Barsbank Lane over the old railway line. The road becomes Star Lane. Cross the main road, and go straight over into Pool Lane, past Statham Post Office. Carry straight on, past Pool Bank Farm, on the right, as the road becomes narrower.

No more than fifty yards after the farm, the road crosses between two ponds - relics of the old course of the River Mersey, before its passage was redirected by the building of the Manchester Ship Canal. The track curves to the right. A footpath leads off dead ahead, with a no entry sign for traffic. The footpath is cobbled and, to the left, is the huge arch of the Thelwall Viaduct. After about fifty yards, the path forks. Head to the right.

Along the right hand side of the path, there is a narrow stretch of water, half-hidden by trees. This is part of one of the old loops of the Mersey, and two stranded barges, dating back to the Mersey and Irwell Navigation, lie in it. The path leads on to the edge of the Manchester Ship Canal, where it all but peters out. On the opposite side, there are the wide flat plateaux of earth, or 'eyes', resulting from the building of the canal. Follow the canal bank to the left with care as there are no railings and a steep drop, and the path comes out at Statham Lane. Turn left into the lane, and follow Pool Lane, Star Lane, and Barsbank Lane back up the hill to the Bridgewater Canal.

Back to the main walk. Follow the Bridgewater Canal towpath out of Lymm to Ditchfield's Bridge, where it goes under the A56. At this point leave the canal, and turn right. It is just over a quarter of a mile to the turning to Eagle Brow, this time on the left, leading down to The Spread Eagle and the centre of Lymm village.

WALK 21: DUNHAM PARK

Waterway: Bridgewater Canal

Distance: 6 miles

Start: Agden Bridge. Map reference: 716/867

Map: OS Pathfinder 740

How to get there: From junction 7 on the M56, take the A56 towards Warrington for three and a half miles, then turn right into the B5159 and follow it to where it goes under the canal. By bus from Warrington, take the 37 service to the junction with the B5159.

This walk is about six miles long, and takes in one of the north west's finest parks, and a stretch of waterway which, for all its apparent tranquility, was the scene of one of the country's worst canal disasters in recent years. In 1971, the Bridgewater Canal aqueduct over the River Bollin burst, almost destroying the embankment with the force of water. The Bridgewater Canal has no locks, and there was consequently an immense amount of pressure behind the burst. Stop planks were put in to block the canal, but so much damage had been done that it was unclear whether the breach would ever be repaired. Fortunately, a concrete channel was built by the Manchester Ship Canal Company, with repairs costing £125,000, and the canal was re-opened in 1973.

Start the walk at Agden. From junction 7 on the M56, it is just about three and a half miles along the A56 towards Warrington to the junction with the B5159. Turn right, and follow the narrow road as it winds its way under the Bridgewater Canal.

The Walk:

The towpath is on the far side. Head east, and Agden Wharf soon appears on the opposite bank. It sells canal books and souvenirs, as well as provisions. The countryside to the left slopes down towards the River Bollin and, further on, the Manchester Ship Canal which, along this section, follows the old line of the Mersey valley.

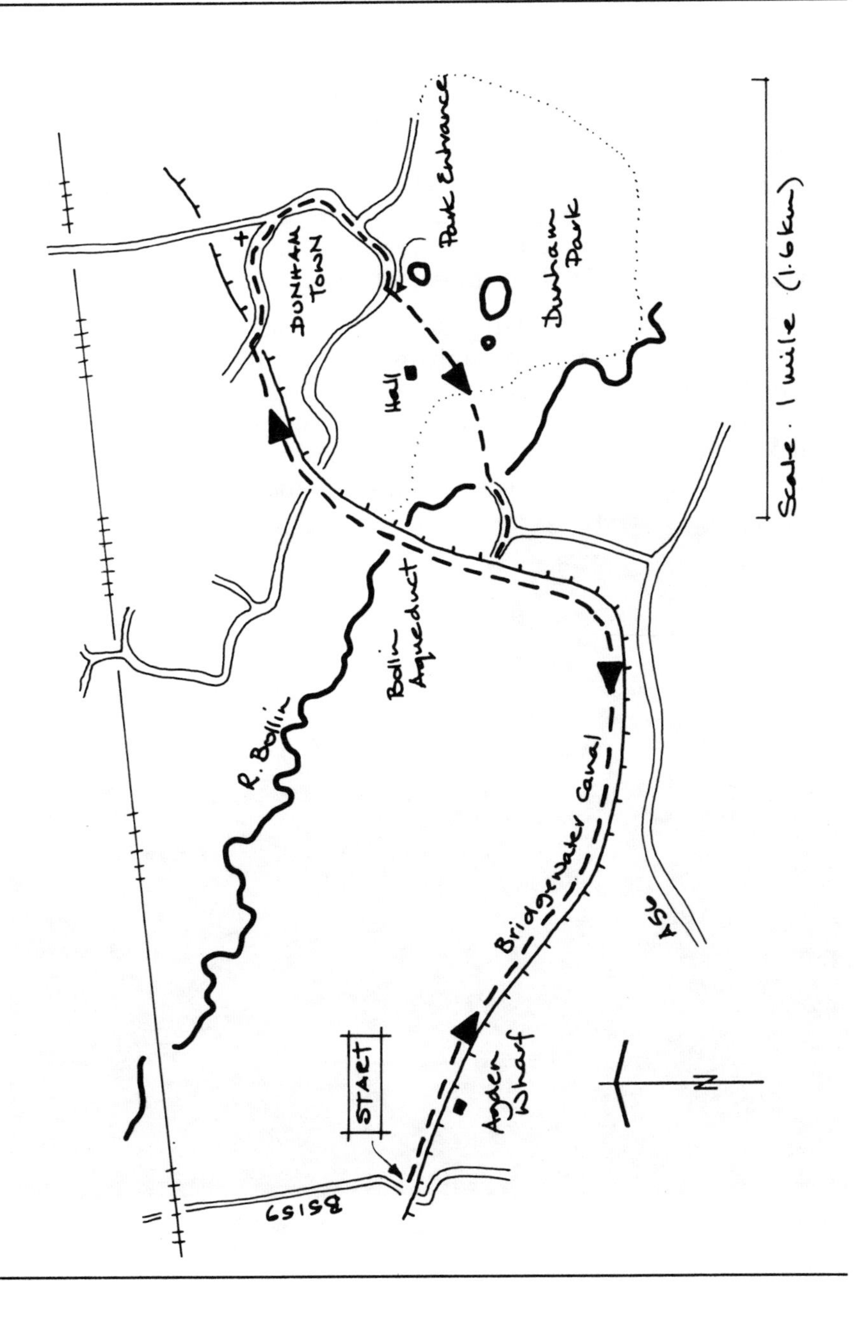
Park Entrance
Dunham Park
DUNHAM TOWN
Hall
Bollin Aqueduct
R. Bollin
Bridgewater Canal
A56
START
Agden Wharf
B5159
N
Scale: 1 mile (1.6km)

After Agden Bridge (26), the canal begins a gradual curve to the left towards the Bollin aqueduct. After crossing a narrow lane, the canal crosses the aqueduct. From the top, the village on the right hand side is Bollington (not to be confused with its much larger namesake, near Macclesfield), and the thick woodland beyond is part of Dunham Park. Just beyond the aqueduct, the canal runs close by the grounds of the park, before crossing over Dunham Underbridge. For those seeking refreshments, it is just under a mile from here along the road, to the left, to the pretty Vine Inn in Dunham Woodhouses.

At bridge 27, leave the towpath, and take the road over the bridge. It is a couple of hundred yards to Dunham Town. At the church, turn right, and follow the road for a couple of hundred yards to where it meets the road around the perimeter of Dunham Park. Turn right, and it is a short distance to the park entrance. The path leads through the wooded deerpark, past a pond with ducks and geese to the front of the hall.

Dunham Massey Hall. (Reproduced by kind permission of The National Trust)

Dunham Hall is on the site of a Norman castle, and was built in the mid- 18th century for the 2nd Earl of Warrington. Just beyond the hall are the attractive courtyard and stable block, which contain a cafeteria and a craft shop. The track leads downhill from here, past the water mill, which is used these days to power wood-turning lathes, and the obelisk on the left hand side, often hidden by trees.

Outside the grounds, follow the path leading between two low-lying meadows with cattle grazing. On the right hand side, there is a good view of the Bollin aqueduct. Bearing in mind how flat the countryside is, one can imagine just how frightening it must have been when the embankment gave way. It is just over quarter of a mile to the bridge across the River Bollin. On the right is the elegant Bollington Mill, which was built in the 1850s, and is currently being converted into flats.

Over the bridge is the village of Bollington, with its pretty pub, 'The Swan with Two Nicks' which serves good food. Shortly after the pub, a narrow lane runs off to the right heading slightly up hill. Follow this, as it curves around to the right, then heads downhill to go under the canal. On the far side, turn left, and take the path up to the canal, and rejoin the towpath. It is about two miles from here back to Agden, and the start of the walk.

WALK 22: COMPSTALL

Waterway: Compstall Navigation

Distance: About 2 miles

Start: Compstall car park. Map reference: 965/909

Map: OS Pathfinder 724

How to get there: From Stockport, take the A626 towards Glossop, turn in to the B6104 down to Compstall. By bus from Stockport, take the 383 or 384 service.

There are all manner of walks around the remains of the Compstall Navigation as, since 1968, it has formed the centre piece of the Etherow Valley Country Park - one of the first in Britain. I have chosen to include a short walk, with a possible extension, as there is only a brief stretch of the navigation that can still be followed.

Start the walk from the car park at Compstall. Head east out of Stockport, on the A626 towards Glossop. Shortly after climbing up the hill out of Marple Bridge, turn left into the B6104 Compstall Road. After less than a mile, the road goes through the centre of Compstall village. Turn right into George Street, and the car park is on the right.

In the 19th century, Compstall became the home of the Andrew family, who built Compstall Mill in the 1820s. In 1824, the first cloth was spun at the mill. Soon, manual spinning was replaced by water-powered looms, driven by the mill's 'Lilly Wheel'.

The Walk:

From the car park, turn left past the warden's office, and follow the path that runs alongside the canal basin. Canada geese, mallards and tufted ducks are all commonly found along this stretch. It is thickly wooded, and in the distance, there are the steep slopes of Ernocroft Wood. The path crosses several little streams and feeders that lead into the waterway. Soon, the basin narrows, and the line of the navigation begins.

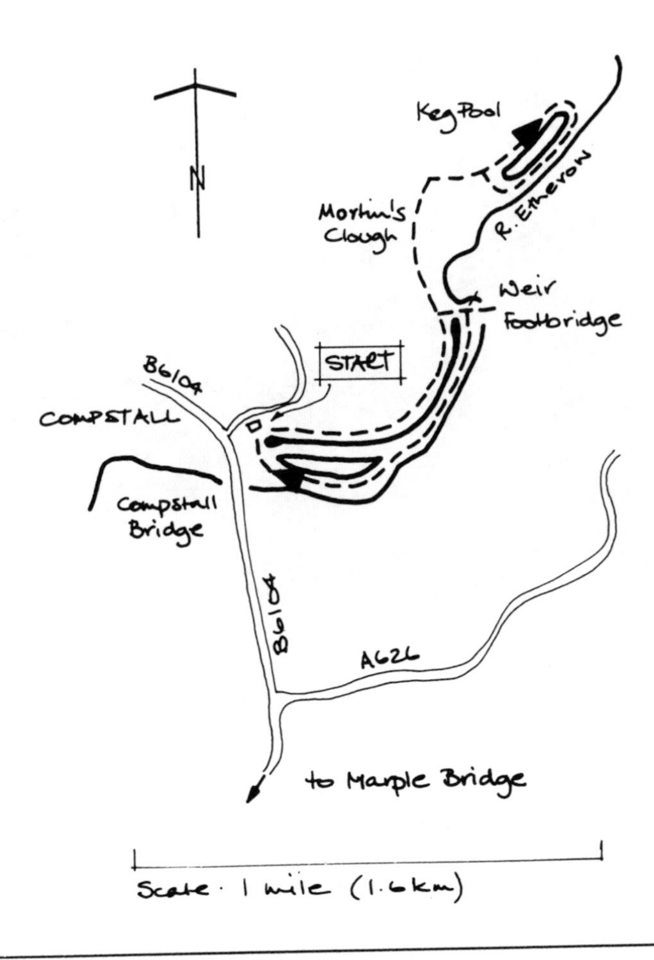

Although the area has been landscaped, many old features of the navigation can still be clearly made out. The path joins another track. Turn right, and follow the path signposted towards The Keg. To the left of the path, there is a steep, wooded bank, and the navigation is on the right. On the other side of the canal, further down the bank, is the River Etherow, with pine woods beyond it. No more than a quarter of a mile after joining this path, there is the first bridge across the navigation.

It is interesting to note the construction of the canal, with the banks

The start of the Compstall Navigation

built in the manner of dry stone walls. It is also said to have a flagged bed. The valley becomes much narrower, as the navigation follows the Etherow upstream. The path curves gradually to the left, as the navigation comes to an end. It forms another basin, and there is an overflow channel on the opposite side to drain excess water into the river. Follow the path around the basin, past the little brick hut, which is where the level of the navigation is controlled. Straight ahead, the path leads to a bridge over the river.

A short distance upstream, the Etherow goes over a substantial weir, which is stepped and semi-circular. The weir was constructed to generate a build-up of water to drive the mill machinery. At one time, planks could be put in at the top of the weir to increase the level even more.

For the shorter walk, return along the path towards the brick hut. Opposite, a path leads off to the left. Follow this path across a wooden bridge over the overflow channel. The path runs between the navigation and the river.

To extend the walk, follow the path beyond the brick hut, around the basin, to where a path leads off to the right, heading uphill. Keep on the path to where it forks into two. Take the right hand fork, and follow the path through the woodland of Mortin Clough. The path bends to the left, then forks again. Follow the right hand path to The Keg Pool, as it curves gradually to the right.The pool was George Andrew's private fishing ground, as he and his family bought the land as far upstream as Keg Wood. There is a path around the pretty pool.

To get back to the start of the walk, go back along the path to the pool, and carry on as if going back to the upper basin on the navigation, but this time take the high level path branching off to the right. This leads through the deciduous woodland, before dropping down to near the start of the navigation. From here, turn right, and it is a short walk back to the car park, and the start of the walk.

WALK 23: MARPLE

Waterway: Peak Forest Canal

Distance: 6 miles

Start: Top of the Marple flight. Map reference: 961/844

Map: OS Pathfinder 741

How to get there: From Stockport, take the A626, then turn into the B6101 towards New Mills. Just before the canal, turn right into Lockside which leads to the top of the Marple flight. By bus from Stockport, take the 363 Stockport – New Mills service.

This walk is a little over six miles, and follows well-made paths all of the way. Even the best paths can be muddy in winter, but strong shoes should be perfectly adequate. It is rather unfortunate that the last mile or so should be alongside roads, but the delightful wooded scenery more than makes up for it. After all, Benjamin Outram, and the other canal builders were not thinking of walkers when they designed the routes their waterway should follow!

From the centre of Marple, take the B6101 Stockport Road towards Strines and New Mills. Just before it crosses the canal, turn right into Lockside, and follow it up to a steep bridge. This is the junction of the Macclesfield canal and the Peak Forest Canal. The bridge (1) is the first on the Macclesfield Canal, and has two curving slopes to allow horses to change from one towpath to another.

The Walk:

To the east of the bridge is the Peak Forest Canal, and this its highest point. Take the path heading downhill to Marple, and the first lock is very close. This is lock 16, the highest of the Marple flight's sixteen locks that drop the canal by 209 feet to the Marple aqueduct. With an average depth of over 13 feet, the locks are very deep, and lower the canal dramatically. The Marple flight should be negotiated with some care, and a sign on the far side of the lock instructs canal users to start filling

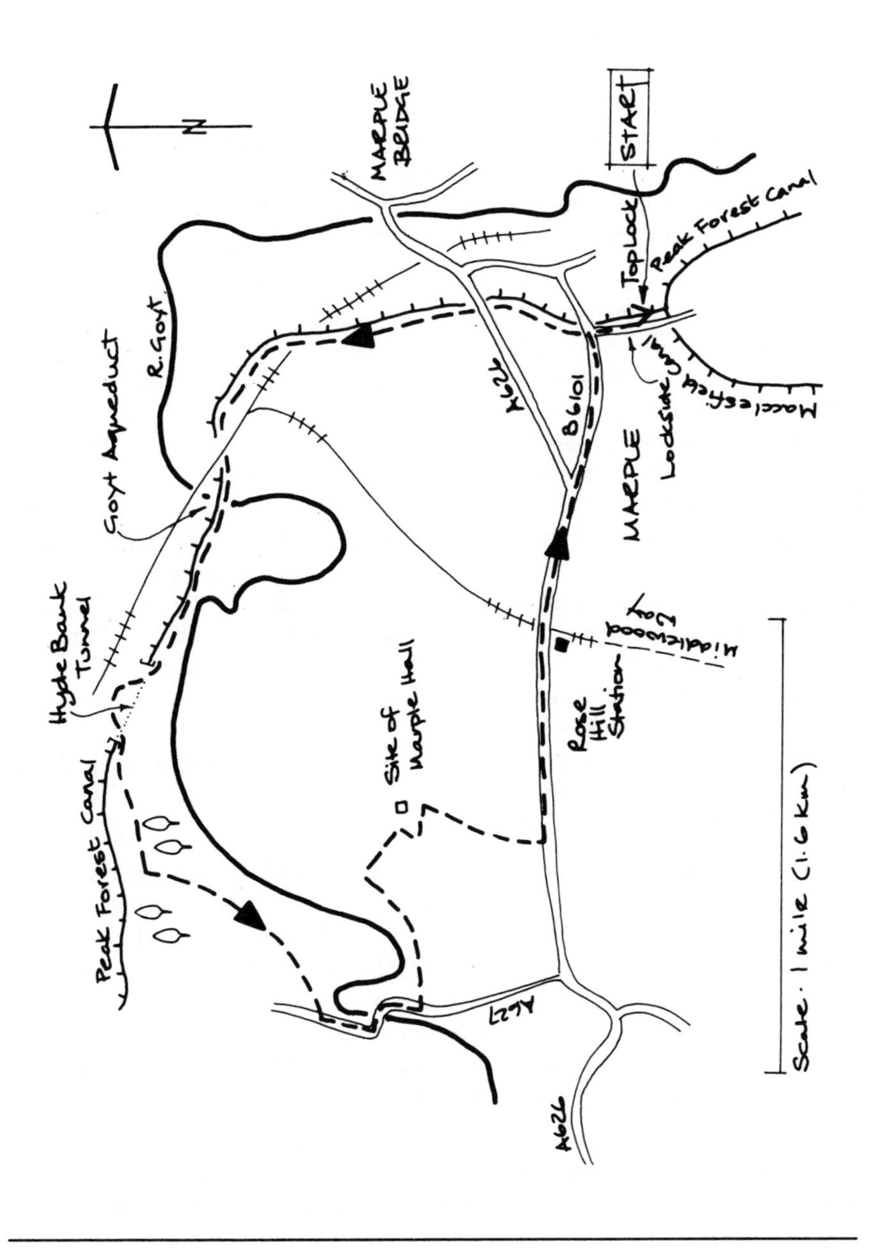
N
MARPLE BRIDGE
START
Top Lock
Peak Forest Canal
Macclesfield Canal
Lockside
MARPLE
B6101
A626
R. Goyt
Goyt Aqueduct
Hyde Bank Tunnel
Peak Forest Canal
Site of Marple Hall
Rose Hill Station
Middlewood Way
A627
A626
Scale: 1 mile (1.6 km)

the next lock before emptying lock 16 and to follow this pattern for the full length of the flight.

All of the locks here, are similar design: single top gate, double bottom gates, with a stone footbridge immediately after it. There are short pounds between the locks and some spread out width-ways to provide sufficent capacity - after all, if a pound were no longer or wider than a lock it would drain completely each time a boat went downhill out of it- equally it would flood each time a boat locked down into it.

Between locks 16 and 15, the pound extends a long way out on the opposite side. There is a similar extension between locks 15 and 14, which is thick with reed beds. Lock 13 takes the canal under the B6101. This is known as 'Posset Bridge', as Samuel Oldknow had given his workman a posset of ale each for completing it on time. It is alongside this stretch of the canal that Oldknow built his limekilns and, just beyond lock 13, there used to be a branch of the canal running off to the right to enable coal and limestone to be unloaded. Although about half of the lime produced in the kilns was used locally, the rest was carried away by boat. The towpath goes down a narrow slope, through an arch, and under the bridge. Just before the arch on the right hand side and slightly higher up, there is a set of steps that appears to lead into the lock chamber itself. In fact, it comes out beside the locks' imposing bottom gates. On the other side of the road, the canal bends gently to the right. Looking back at the bridge, there are two arches - one for the lock and one for the sluices. It is another short pound before lock 12. In the distance, one can see the hills around the Etherow Valley. Lock 12 is one of the prettiest in the flight.

Just before lock 11, there are great stone slabs between the bank and the towpath, and the sluice channel goes under them. Between locks 11 and 10, the sluice is open, running to the left of the towpath, and cascading into the pound below lock 10, opposite Lockside Mill, which was once the property of Samuel Oldknow, and is now a converted wharf. Lock 9 is immediately followed by Station Road, the A626 to Glossop. Take the path up to the main road, cross over the canal, and cross the road to join the towpath which is now on the opposite side.

The path is well made and runs alongside a stone wall, with beech trees and thick woodland behind it. The canal sweeps round to the left, and it is not far to lock 8. To the right, beyond tennis courts, there is a splendid view of the Pennines. The canal is wider after lock 8, appearing to fork into two. It is simply a wide pound, with a reedy island in the middle. The towpath is in excellent condition, and great efforts have been made to keep the canal in good order. It is particularly important that this stretch of canal should be well-kept since, if it were allowed to flood or leak, it could be potentially very dangerous to the people of Marple.

Locks at Marple

Just after lock 7, the sluice rushes out through a great, round culvert. There is yet another short pound at lock 6. Thick deciduous woodland slopes downhill to Brabyns Park, to the right of the path, which nestles in a bend of the River Goyt. After lock 6, there are thick reed beds along the opposite bank. The opposite side of lock 5 appears to be an island, betweeen the canal and the sluice channel. To the right of lock 5, the Manchester to New Mills railway can be seen down the hill, before it goes under the canal. Before lock 4, there is a wide bowl of a pound. Then the canal bends to the left, and the countryside appears to drop away more and more steeply as lock 3 is approached.

After lock 2, the canal is densely wooded on both banks and the last lock in the flight is soon reached. Beside lock 1 is a delightful stone cottage, and this heralds the start of the Lower Peak Forest that continues at this level to Dukinfield, where it joins the Ashton Canal. The canal kinks to the right, under a stone bridge. Cross over the top, as the towpath changes sides. It is only about a hundred yards to the great arches of the Manchester to New Mills railway viaduct - it is some indication of how steeply the canal descends, since a few locks back one could look down on the railway.

Under the viaduct, the path bends slightly to the right. The canal becomes very narrow, and crosses Marple Aqueduct - one of the great triumphs of engineering from the canal age. The aqueduct has three arches, and carries the canal almost a hundred feet above the River Goyt. It was opened in 1800, and was designed by the Peak Forest Canal Engineer, Benjamin Outram. To reduce the weight of the structure, Outram constructed voids in the shoulder of the arches. A particularly aesthetic feature resulted from Outram's decision to build the parapet in a different coloured gritstone from the rest of the aqueduct.

On the right of the aqueduct are the high arches of the railway, while the dense trees down below to the left almost wholly obscure the Goyt in summer. It is interesting to note that the opposite side of the aqueduct, the canal goes through a narow channel between steep walls, and under a small bridge. After the bridge, the land rises steeply to the right, and falls away to the left. Down the slope by the towpath, great stone buttresses support the canal from below. The canal bends slightly to the right before entering Hyde Bank Tunnel, which is 308 yards long.

The towpath goes up along the left hand side of the tunnel entrance, rising up to the roof of the tunnel. About half way up is an old stone water trough for the horses, which would have been unhitched from boats and led over the tunnel roof to the other side, while the crew 'legged' their way through. The path is joined by another from the right. Carry straight on from here and there is a fine view of Manchester from its south east side. The path goes downhill past Hyde Bank Farm. It gets wider, and winds to the left.

The path forks about a hundred yards beyond the farm. Take the left hand path, heading downhill, which comes out by the end of the tunnel.

The path crosses over the opening, and curves round to the right. There is a large factory ahead, but just before it take a path off to the left. It is marked 'To Chadkirk'. Go up three steps, follow the path through a wood, as it crosses small wooded bridges, and runs parallel to a small brook down the slope on the right hand side.

The path is well marked - follow the main line of it, rather than any of the smaller ones branching off it. A row of large yew trees line the left hand side of the path. After dropping down gradually, the path comes out in a clearing, where it appears to divide into three. Take the path curving downhill to the right. It goes down steps to a junction. Follow the path to the left. On the right of the path is a wooden fence, and the lush meadows of Chadkirk. The path comes out into a small road, with trees running along its left side. Turn left into the road. For those interested in architecture, just over half a mile to the right is Chadkirk's 14th century chapel, which was built on the site of a monastic cell, founded by St Chad. The area surrounding Chadkirk once belonged to the Davenport family who, in the 1570s built Goyt Hall, a couple of miles further down the river from Chadkirk.

The small road pases a couple of farms and comes out into the A627 Otterspool Road. Turn left, and the Goyt runs along the left side, making two great 180 degree bends. Follow the road over the stone arched bridge across the Goyt. Across the bridge is a garden centre and, just beyond it, a stile leads off to the left. Follow a well made track crossing a field to a gate. The path rises gradually through a wood after crossing a stream running down to the Goyt. Keep to the main path as it climbs through woodland. Below, to the left, the Goyt twists and turns through its last stages before joining the Tame at Stockport to form the Mersey.

The path leads right towards Marple Hall School and its playing fields, and follows the perimeter fence. On the left, the land continues to drop away sharply down ot the river. The view to the left looks across the broad Goyt valley and its rich pastures across to the steep tree-lined slopes up to Romiley. Follow the path through a gate, into small wooded park, which is the site of Marple Hall, demolished in 1959. It was the home of the Bradshaw family since 1606. Henry Bradshaw II was actively involved in the Civil War, while John Bradshaw was Lord President at the trial of Charles I and first signatory on the death warrant. There is nothing left of the hall, apart from a large stone with

1658 inscribed on it. The path comes out, through a gate, into Marple Hall Drive. Follow this until it meets the main Stockport Road.

Turn left, past 'The Railway', and cross the bridge over the single track line to Rose Hill Station, where the line now terminates. The road enters the centre of Marple. Turn right into Church Lane, and follow it for half a mile past the Carver Theatre to where it rises to cross the Macclesfield Canal. Go over the bridge and take the path down to the towpath on the left. It is about a hundred yards from bridge number one, and the junction with the Peak Forest Canal. Just before the junction, the canal becomes very narrow, and presumably there was once a stop lock here, in the days when canals were owned by private companies, to ensure that craft passing through Marple Locks on the Peak Forest Canal could not take water from the Macclesfield. On the left, there is the old wharf, and the path rises up the stone sets ot the top of the bridge and junction, which is the start of the walk.

Canal Notes

It is worth considering, however, the great many other canal schemes, proposed during the Industrial Revolution, that never left the drawing board. How would the face of the north west have been changed if a canal linking Sheffield with the Peak Forest (proposed in 1852) or the proposed extension of the Bridgewater into Stockport had been built? There were other canals, too, which have now totally disappeared from view. The five mile stretch of the Ashton Canal that went from Fairfield, east of Manchester to Heaton Norris just north of Stockport, was abandoned in 1982 and has since been filled in. Now there is little to suggest it ever existed, except for rows of streets that all stop along a given line for no apparent reason.

Benjamin Outram, one of the founders of Butterley Ironworks in Derbyshire, was appointed to work as engineer on the Peak Forest Canal, which would link up Derbyshire's limestone quarries with Ashton, Hyde and ultimately, Manchester. The main purpose of the canal was to provide lime and serve the collieries in the Hyde area.

Local entrepreneur, Samuel Oldknow was elected to the committee responsible for the canal. He had plans to build a cotton mill further south at Mellor, and limekilns at Marple. Best known for the pioneering the manufacture of muslin, Oldknow contributed substantially to the building of the canal.

Lack of funds hampered the building of the canal, following the Peak Forest Act being passed in 1794. By March 1797, work was postponed until sufficient capital had been raised from the shareholders. With money being in short supply, a decision was taken to build the lower section, and the aqueduct, but to connect this low level with the upper level further south by a tramway, rather than the 16 locks which stand there now.

Transporting cargoes of limestone, from quarries at Dovehols to Marple and beyond was clearly hindered by the tramway, as it was necessary to take the cargo from a boat to a wagon, then onto a boat again. To try and improve the situation, a system of containers was devised. Iron boxes, each carrying 2 tons, worked up and down the tramway, but a more elegant solution was still badly needed.

The tramway remained in use until 1807, running alongside the canal, well after the locks had been constructed and were in use. The committee had more to worry about than raising enough money to build locks, since they faced stiff competition from local mill owners who were concerned that they may be deprived of existing water levels. Outram had left the scheme by 1801, and Thomas Brown was appointed engineer to build the sixteen locks, which finally cost £27,000 to construct, and were opened in October 1804.

Although the canal never made great profits, it remained in commercial use well in to this century. The canal survived the Second World War, but disaster struck soon after, and was to strike again. Following the nationalisation of the waterways in 1948, the canal received little maintenance, and it became apparent that there was no future for either the Ashton or the Peak Forest Canal below Marple. Commercial traffic had come to a standstill by 1958, and by 1961, the Ministry of Transport was planning to do away with several stretches of canal.

Strenuous efforts were made to persuade the ministry to restore the canal to its former glory, and the Inland Waterways association organised a rally and a public meeting. The cold winter of 1961-62 brought the matter to a head. The stone work at Marple aqueduct was weakened by freezing, and water seeped out. The entire structure was damaged, and the canal had to be closed off. To repair the aqueduct would have cost £35,000, while demolition would be substantially cheaper. The local councils agreed that the aqueduct, being of great historic interest, should be saved, and that money should be found to allow its complete restoration. The winter of 1962-63, the coldest on record, did even more damage, and required even more money to be raised. The aqueduct was duly repaired, but the Marple flight of locks, having lain disused for so long, had fallen into very poor condition. Volunteers began to work on Marple locks. With little in the way of funds and personnel, and with the continual problem of vandalism and the dumping of rubbish, the volunteers finally restored both the Ashton and Peak Forest Canals by March 1974. The canal was officially opened by Denis Howell MP, and there is a plaque beside Marple top lock.

With the restoration of Marple locks and aqueduct, the Cheshire Ring is complete. Enthusiasts can now navigate, from Manchester, along the Bridgewater Canal, the Trent and Mersey, the Macclesfield, the Peak Forest and then the Ashton Canal, and back to the start. It is a classic journey, providing contrasts between urban and rural landscapes, revealing some fo the most imaginative engineering feats of the industrial revolution, and showing the very individual solutions produced by the different canal builders. In fact, the route is so well-travelled by pleasure craft, today, that it is hard to imagine it was so nearly lost forever.

WALK 24: STRINES TO NEW MILLS

Waterway: Peak Forest Canal

Distance: 6 miles

Start: Strines Station. Map reference: 978/865

Map: OS Pathfinder 741

How to get there: Head out of Marple on the B6101 towards New Mills, and turn left into Strines. By bus from Stockport, take the 363 New Mills service.

This walk is just under six miles, but passes through countryside that seems perpetually muddy, so boots or wellingtons are essential.

Start the walk from Strines Station. Climbing out of Marple on the road to New Mills (B6101), turn left after two miles into a small, winding road. To the left is the enormous chimney of the textile mill at Strines, and the road then passes a reservoir, much frequented by anglers, with a bizarre, octagonal dovecote (on a small island) surmounted by an elaborate weather vane. The road bends past Whitecroft Farm, and a steep cobbled track leads up to Strines Station.

The Walk:

Go under the Manchester to New Mills railway line. Follow the path uphill. It is a well-made path and, although steep, is rarely slippery. To the left, the land dips away steeply down a tree-lined bank. Beyond it are the small farms dotted along the sides of Mellor Moor. On the right, one can see across to Marple Ridge, and the square-towered folly of Lyme Cage in the distance. After less than a mile, the path rises seeeply and comes out at Brook Bottom. The Fox Inn is on the left, in this tiny hamlet, and serves food and Robinson's beers.

Follow the road round to the right for a couple of hundred yards, and a stony track branches off to the right. It drops down steeply to another hamlet, Hague Bar, between dry stone walls. After about half a mile, it winds down to the main road. Cross over, and follow the track down

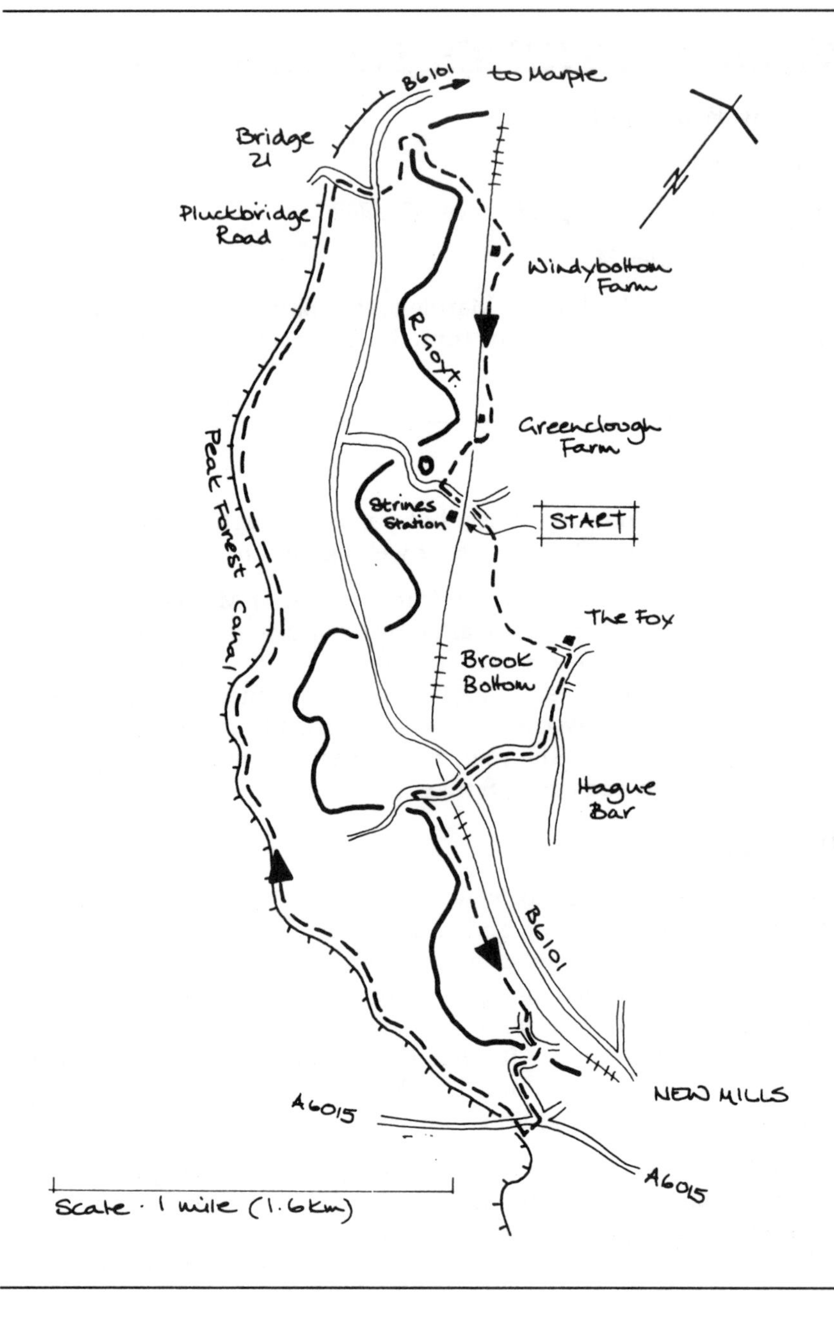
B6101
to Marple
Bridge 21
Pluckbridge Road
Windybottom Farm
R. Goyt
Greenclough Farm
Strines Station
START
Peak Forest Canal
The Fox
Brook Bottom
Hague Bar
B6101
NEW MILLS
A6015
A6015
N
Scale · 1 mile (1.6Km)

on the opposite side, over the railway, and contine for another two hundred yards. A stile leads to a good path on the left. The path comes out by the River Goyt - a small river that rises near the Cat and Fiddle and forms the River Mersey at its confluence with the River Tame in Stockport. The river is delightfully wooded, and horses graze in the pastures that slope gently down to its banks.

After crossing another stile, there is a stone path leading away from the river to the left. Follow it up a gradual incline, and then it drops down to a stile. Over the stile, there is a derelict barn; follow the track to the left hand side of the barn, through a gate and out onto a small road. This is not the prettiest part of the walk. For two hundred yards, the road is lined with industry, and then a path appears on the right. It leads down to a wooden bridge over the Goyt, and is so wooded that the surrounding industry disappears from view. This very pretty bridge crosses two channels of the river on either side of an island, and then a small concrete bridge crosses a very narrow channel, which was presumably once used as a mill race.

The path winds to the right, up stone steps, and the landscape becomes industrial again - but not for long. It open out onto a yard, but you follow the left hand side over an old weighbridge to a juncion. Coming out at a tarmac road, turn left, and follow it uphill for a hundred yards to a main road. Cross over, and take the short cut, down Victoria Street, to the Peak Forest Canal. Turn right onto the towpath, and follow the canal under bridge 28. Around here, the air is full of sweet smells that take one back to childhood. The reason is that just beyond the bridge is the Swizzels Mattlow Sweet Factory, where 'Love Hearts' and all manner of sherbets and gob-stoppers come from.

Within a hundred yards the canal is in attractive countryside. The land slopes away steeply to the right, down to the railway and the Goyt beyond. By one bend, there is a sluice next to the towpath for draining excess water away into the Goyt. Following a high line to Marple, there are several points where the canal can be emptied into the river. The canal winds along the contour line, under bridges 27 and 26, and into a wooded stretch. There is a bend to the right, as the canal crosses Disley Tunnel over the railway, and one of the canal's curious swingbridges appears. Bridge 25 is made of iron, and is opened by turning the winding gear with a lock key.

Just beyond the bridge there is a long overflow channel beside the towpath, taking water down the steep hillside to the Goyt. The next bridge (24) is also a swing bridge, set in a quiet stretch of the canal. After bridge 23 the canal crosses a path from Strines to Marple Ridge. Following bridge 22, another swing bridge, this section of the canal becomes more open with views over to the large cross on top of Mellor Moor, and the square-towered church of St Thomas at Mellor. At bridge 21 take the path leading away from the towpath, and follow it downhill until it joins a tarmac track, Pluckbridge Road. Keep going downhill until the track comes out at the main road.

Cross over, and follow the steep track down, until it becomes narrow and wooded. The path bends to the left, and comes out by a superb stone bridge spanning the Goyt. The bridge seems to rise naturally out of the great slabs of rock beside the river. Over the bridge, the path rises to a junction. Take the track to the right past the small group of farms and houses that make up Strawberry Hill. Follow it round as it winds under the railway, and comes out at Windybottom Farm.

The track can get very muddy beyond the farm, where it runs parallel to the railway. After just over half a mile, it slopes down through woodland and joins another path. Follow it as it rises to the left for a short distance, and then turn right into Greenclough Farm. The path goes up to the left at the farm, before crossing over the railway. From here it is about a quarter of a mile downhill to a tarmac road. A house on the left has an elaborate series of pools leading to a stream up to and under the path. Turn left, and Strines Station is a couple of hundred yards away.

The shallow, but picturesque Peak Forest Canal was opened in 1800, and was fully operational (following the construction of Marple Locks) by 1804. In its day, the canal was a main transport route for coal, lime and limestone; and could link up with Manchester and the north via the Ashton Canal, and later with the Midlands via its junction with the Macclesfield Canal at Marple. The growth of the railway network led to increased competition, but the Peak Forest Canal managed to hold its own by introducing toll reductions. This was not to last. By 1844, the company gave way to an offer from the Sheffield, Ashton under Lyne and Manchester railway to take over the canal and its debts on a permanent lease. By the end of the last century, trade had declined, with goods being transported on the railways running parallel with the canal.

WALK 25: FURNESS VALE TO NEW MILLS

Waterway: Peak Forest Canal

Distance: Just over 3 miles

Start: Furness Vale, where the road crosses the canal. Map reference: 009/836

Map: OS Outdoor Leisure Map. The Peak District: The Dark Peak

How to get there: It is nine miles to Furness Vale from Stockport along the A6. By bus, take the 198, or 199 Stockport to Buxton services.

This is one of the shorter walks - a Sunday afternoon stroll which passes through pretty scenery, and is only a little over three miles. There are plenty of places where refreshments may be bought, and the paths are well-made and easy to follow.

Start the walk from Furness Vale. Heading south out of Stockport on the A6 towards Buxton, it is about nine miles to Furness Vale. Turn left at the sign to the station, and it is a very short distance to where the road goes over the Manchester to Buxton railway by a level crossing, then crosses the Peak Forest Canal.

The Walk:

The towpath is on the far side. Cross the bridge (31), and turn to the left.

On the right hand side of the canal runs the River Goyt, and it is along this narrow valley that the main A6, and the two railways from Manchester to Buxton and to Sheffield run close by the two waterways. On either side there are steep hillsides, Chinley Churn to the right, and Black Hill to the left.

Follow the canal for just under half a mile, and then there is Carr Bridge, one of the swing bridges that are common on the Peak Forest, and which often prove hard work for holiday makers. The canal is clean and well-kept, and even though industry is never very far away it runs through some glorious countryside. After Bankend Bridge (29), it is not far to New Mills, which straddles the canal, with New Mills itself on the right and New Mills Newtown to the left, with their separate railway stations on the two different lines.

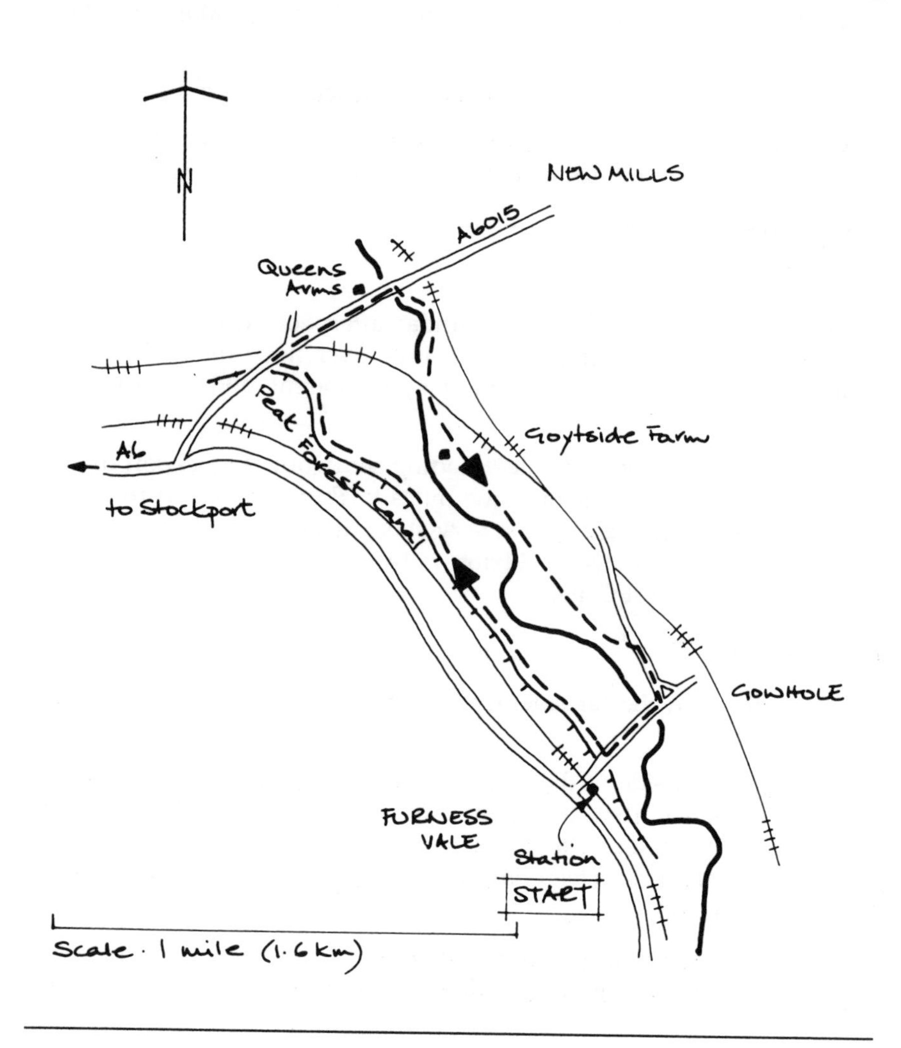

Just before bridge 28, New Mills Marina is on the opposite bank, invariably busy with pleasure craft. At the bridge, leave the towpath, and cross over on to the other side and follow the A6105 for about a quarter of a mile. Go past the Queen's Arms, and cross over the River Goyt. Take the first right on the other side, it is a well-made track that follows the river past a weir, then leads under the railway.

After the railway, the path becomes less defined, but it is easy to follow as it never strays far from the river. Pass Goytside Farm, to the left, and stay on the path that leads straight ahead. Cross a stile, and then head towards another one which is close to a bend in the river. Once over the stile, follow the path for just over a quarter of a mile to where it bends left and there is a gate.

Go through the gate, and onto the road. Turn right, and follow the road down into Gowhole. Where the road forks, keep to the right, and head along Marsh Lane. Follow the road as it crosses the Goyt, and it leads to the bridge over the canal and the start of the walk.

This walk can be extended by joining it to either, or both of two other walks in this book - the one from Furness Vale to Buxworth and Whaley Bridge to the south (Walk 26), and the other from Strines to New Mills to the north (Walk 24). While the former is straightforward, the latter involves following the return journey before the outward one.

WALK 26: WHALEY BRIDGE AND BUXWORTH

Waterway: Peak Forest Canal

Distance: Just under 4 miles

Start: Furness Vale station. Map reference: 009/836

Map: OS Outdoor Leisure Map: The Dark Peak

How to get there: Nine miles south of Stockport on the A6, Furness Vale is set just to the left of the main road. By bus from Stockport, take the 198, or 199 Buxton services.

This is a short walk, just under four miles. The paths are well kept and it is never too far from civilisation. This is a walk for canal enthusiasts, as there are so many aspects of waterway history crammed into this small area. It is an appealling mixture - hills and a river, history and modern day restoration, tourism and memories of an industrial past.

Start the walk from Furness Vale Station. Almost nine miles south of Stockport on the A6, heading towards Buxton, is Furness Vale. Turn left at the sign to Furness Vale Station. The road heads downhill, and the station is on the right.

The Walk:

Cross the Manchester to Buxton railway by the level crossing, and go over the bridge across the Peak Forest Canal.

Go down to the towpath and turn right, away from the bridge. On the left of the towpath, the River Goyt runs close by, and beyond that is the Manchester to Sheffield railway. After half a mile, the canal passes under Greensdeep Bridge (33) The land rises steeply on either side of the canal, and it is easy to see why two railway lines, the A6 and the canal run parallel along this narrow stretch of the Goyt valley. The canal goes under the junction of roads leading to Whaley Bridge and Chapel-en-le-Frith.

The Peak Forest Canal at Whaley Bridge

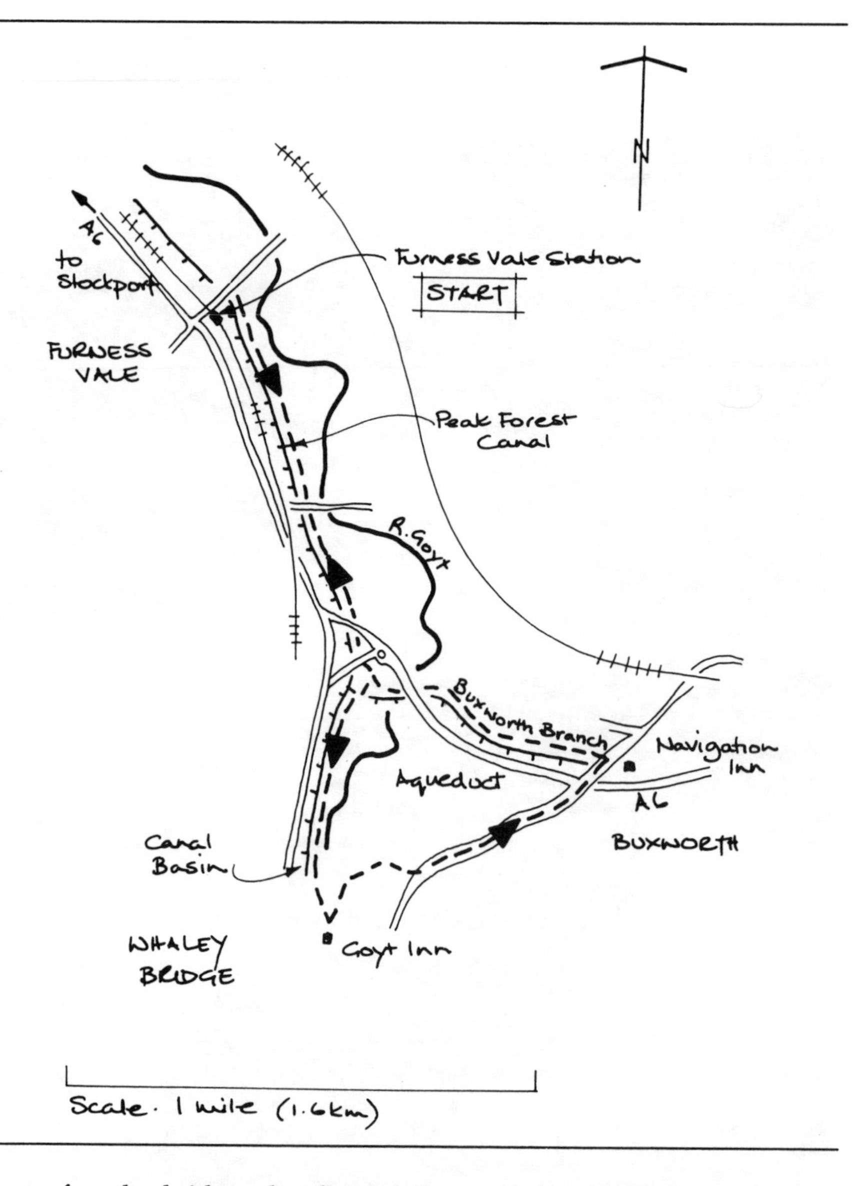

Just after the bridge, the disused Buxworth arm, which is currently being restored, runs off to the left. Cross over the footbridge that runs across the entrance, and follow the branch to Whaley Bridge. It is about half a mile from the junction with the Buxworth arm to Whaley Bridge Basin, the southern terminus of the Peak Forest canal. The towpath leads out into a narrow road. Follow it to a T-junction, with The Goyt Inn on the right. Turn left and cross the River Goyt, and shortly after take a footpath that leads off to the left. The path curves away from the river and rises, bearing round to the right, to join a road, coming out beside a telephone box.

On the road, turn left, and follow it uphill, then down to Buxworth Basin, after crossing over the A6. The road leads up to the Navigation Inn, on the left. Just before the pub, turn left on to the well-made track on the far side of the canal basin that goes on to form the towpath. Follow the towpath for just over half a mile to where it meets the footpath along the Peak Forest canal, by the footbridge. This short stretch runs along an embankment with an aqueduct crossing the River Goyt. Turn right and head back along the towpath to Furness Vale and the start of the walk.

Canal Notes:

In the 1820s, a link was planned between the Peak Forest Canal and the Cromford Canal across the Peak District. It was finally agreed that it would be impossible to build a canal over such steep gradients so a railway line was built instead, from Whaley Bridge to just south of Matlock. Just over thirty miles long, the Cromford and High Peak railway was officially opened in 1833. The line still had to cope with ferociously steep inclines, and a series of inclined planes, and engines were built to take traffic up and down. Closed in 1967, there is little left of the railway now. At Whaley Bridge Basin, however, there is a building at the far end which dates back to the building of the railway, and this was where cargo was transferred from canal to railway.

In its heyday, Buxworth was a bustling canal terminus, and was linked to the limestone quarries at Doveholes by a tramway constructed in 1799. Less than seven miles long, the Peak Forest tramway carried stone down to Buxworth Basin, where it was transferred to canal boats. Horses drew wagons along the line and at Chapel-en-le-Frith an inclined plane was constructed to overcome the gradient. In the 1920s the tramway was abandoned, and Buxworth Basin became disused. By 1931, the name of the little town was officially changed from Bugsworth to Buxworth. Although there is little today to indicate how busy

Buxworth Basin used to be, there is still a narrow section, resembling a lock, where a boat's cargo could be measured. Planks, like those used in a stop lock, would be inserted at either end of the boat, and the weight of the cargo was calculated from the depth of water displaced.

The building of the Cromford and High Peak Railway largely resulted from the close friendship between Richard Arkwright and Samuel Oldknow. Arkwright's operations in the village of Cromford relied on the Cromford Canal while Oldknows's village of Mellor and his lime-kilns at Marple, were by the Peak Forest Canal. Both men felt that the railway would be to their mutual benefit, and Josiah Jessop (whose father was William Jessop, the engineer on the Cromford Canal) was given the task of over-coming gradients as steep as 1 in 7.

The Peak Forest Canal fared rather better than the Cromford, which suffered similarly from the railway boom, but had to be closed due to mining subsidence. Only the top five miles contain water, and it no longer meets up with the junction of the Erewash and Nottingham Canals at Langley Mill.

WALK 27: ADLINGTON TO LYME PARK

Waterway: Macclesfield Canal

Distance: 9 miles

Start: The canal at Adlington. Map reference: 929/802

Map: OS Pathfinder 741

How to get there: Heading south, it is four miles south along the A523 from its junction with the A6 to Adlington. Turn right into the Pott Shrigley road to where it crosses the canal. By bus, take the 201 Manchester to Derby service, and it is just over a mile from the A523 to the start of the walk.

This walk goes across quite mixed terrain, and boots are strongly recommended. There are plenty of interesting diversions, including Adlington Hall near the start of the walk, and Lyme Park, but the walk itself is about nine miles long. It is a particularly pretty rural walk and, remarkably enough, only a few miles outside Stockport. Since the railway alongside the canal has been disused, the walk has become more rural still.

Start the walk from where the Adlington to Pott Shrigley road crosses the Macclesfield canal. Heading south from the junction of the A523 and the A6 at Hazel Grove, go through Poynton and, after four miles, there is a turning to the left to Adlington Station. The road crosses the railway and, a mile later, goes over the Middlewood Way, and then the canal, where it is possible to park.

The Walk:

Take the steps down to the towpath, and follow it under bridge 21. This is a pretty stretch of canal, and I have seen swans here on several occasions. The canal curves to the right, and the towpath is leafy and well-kept. To the left, there is a splendid view of Manchester city centre's tall buildings, with Winter Hill beyond. It is not far from Manchester Airport, and passenger aircraft loom large and low.

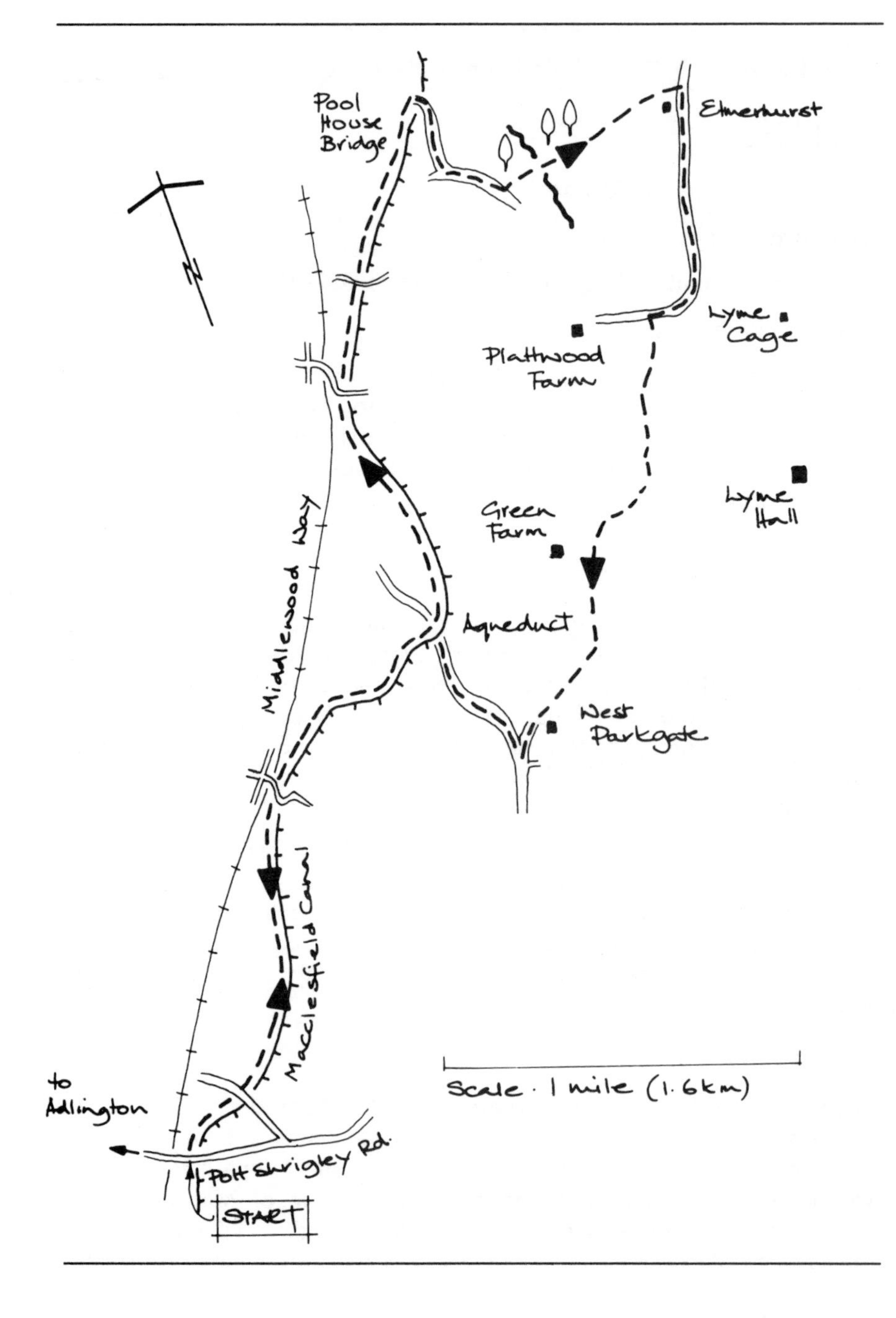
Pool
House
Bridge
Elmerhurst
N
Lyme
Cage
Plattwood
Farm
Green
Farm
Lyme
Hall
Middlewood Way
Aqueduct
West
Parkgate
Macclesfield Canal
to
Adlington
Scale · 1 mile (1·6km)
Pott Shrigley Rd.
START

Woodford Aerodrome is even closer, and this is an excellent vantage point for its air shows.

After bridge 20, the canal bends very close to the disused Marple to Macclesfield railway, which has since been converted into 'The Middlewood Way' - one of several 'linear parks' in the region which follow old railway lines. Bridges 19 and 18 just lead to farms on the higher ground to the right, although beside the latter is 'The Miner's Arms' dating back to the days of coal mining in the Poynton area, an attractive pub which serves good food. The canal then bends to the right, and crosses a road by way of a sturdy, if dripping, aqueduct. Just beyond it, there is a wide drainage channel along the opposite bank, leading excess water down into Poynton Brook.

There is a sharp bend to the left, as the canal follows the contour line. Before passing under an iron footbridge, the canal becomes very narrow, and there are the remains of a swing bridge set into the bank. To the right, the land rises steeply to the hills above Lyme Hall. The canal runs parallel to the old railway which is hidden in a deep cutting to the left. The next bridge (15) is at Higher Poyton, and there is marina beside it on the opposite bank. This part of the canal is an ideal introduction to touring the country's inland waterways as it is both scenic and, for the sixteen miles between Marple and Bosley, there are no locks to negotiate.

Following bridge 14, it is about half a mile to Pool House Bridge (13). Take the path up the side of the bridge, and cross over. There is a stony track leading away from the canal, and a small wood of fir trees ahead to the right. There are often horses in the fields to the left. Follow the track until it comes out a a junction. Take the left hand fork which heads in the direction of the square-towered folly of Lyme Cage, which is thought to have been built for watching hunts. Although there is no record of when it was built, it would seem to be Elizabethan. The track goes through farmland, and is lined by hedges. About half a mile after leaving the canal, there is a small stile to the left - it is easily missed.

Cross the stile, and follow the path along the edge of a field leading down to Middle Cale Wood. There is another stile into the wood. The path winds downhill to the left, and there is a small stream at the bottom which goes into Norbury Brook. Cross over an attractive wooden bridge, and the path rises to a stile that leads out of the wood.

On the other side, there are open fields to the right, while the wood continues for a quarter of a mile on the left side. The path leads to a set of steps built into a sandstone wall, and a stony track beyond it. Ahead are the wooded slopes above Disley and the higher hills of the Pennines' western edge beyond. In some seasons, it is possible to see the Manchester to Buxton railway through the trees.

The path comes out at a gate with a cottage called Elmerhurst on the right. Straight ahead are the deer park and lush grounds around Lyme Hall. The building dates from Elizabethan times, although this is disguised by the Palladian exterior designed by Giacomo Leoni in 1720. Lyme Hall was the house of the Legh family for 60 years, and contains fine examples of Grinling Gibbons carvings. It is about a mile and a half beyond the gate, and is well-signposted.

Said to be the largest house in Cheshire, Lyme Park is built on the site of an older building, referred to in documents dating to 1465. The original structure was built by Sir Piers Legh VII in 1541. It would seem that Sir Piers house was E-shaped, as were so many Elizabethan houses, with a tower (taken down by Lewis Wyatt in 1810, and rebuilt some distance from the house).

For the purpose of this walk, however, turn right after the gate and take the well-made track that rises gently uphill. To the right there is grazing land, and there is woodland on the left. Over the next mile, the track climbs gradually up to Platt Wood Farm. A couple of hundred yards before the farm, there is a path leading off to the left. Follow this less well-made path as it crosses a wide track and, after a stile, leads gently downhill. From here, the canal is visible to the right. Beyond are Alderley Edge, and the Welsh hills in the distance. Do not take the path leading off right to Green Farm, but stay on the main path beside a fence and leading parallel to a tarmac track slightly further donwhill to the right.

After a stile over a stone wall, the two paths converge. Turn left, and follow the gravel track down past West Gate (to Lyme Park), and over a brook. The path is fenced, and comes out on a narrow road. Turn right, and follow the road as it winds down the hill for half a mile, alongside the brook. Go under the canal aqueduct, and there is a path on the right leading up to the towpath. From the top, it is about a mile and a half back to the bridge at Adlington.

The Cage, Lyme Park

If time permits, nearby Adlington Hall is well worth a visit, but it is usualy only open on Sundays. The Hall has belonged to the Legh family since 1315. The Great Hall was built between 1450 and 1505, with additions in 1581, and the construction of the Georgian south facade in 1757. There are charming gardens, with a yew walk, an avenue of lime trees, a shell cottage and a rotunda.

WALK 28: BOLLINGTON

Waterway: Macclesfield Canal

Distance: 7 miles

Start: Bollington Aqueduct over the B5090. Map reference: 933/779

Map: OS Pathfinder 759

How to get there: Bollington is about two miles along the B5090 from its junction with A523 Stockport to Macclesfield road. By bus from either Macclesfield or Stockport, take the E8 service.

Boots are best for this walk, as it does not keep to the towpath. It is about seven miles long, and can be extended by following the signs to Pott Shrigley. There are several steep sections, so it is not advisable for those expecting a gentle afternoon stroll. There are also some sections where dogs are not welcome, unless on a lead.

Start the walk from Bollington Aqueduct. Heading north from Macclesfield, on the A523 road to Stockport, turn right after two miles, into the B5090 to Bollington. After about 2 miles the road winds round to the aqueduct. It is possible to park just beyond the aqueduct.

The Walk:

Climb a steep flight of stone steps leading up from the right hand pavement, just before the aqueduct. At the top, 60 ft above the road, there is a path that curves round to the canal bank. A gate leads to the towpath and on the opposite bank there is a timber yard. Turn right, and go under a stone-arched bridge (27)

The canal is in very good condition here, and great efforts have been made to ensure the towpath and canal banks are well-kept. About 200 yards after the bridge, there is a milestone by the towpath. It reads: '18 miles from Hall Green' (the junction with the Trent and Mersey, near Kidsgrove), while the reverse shows that it is 8 miles to Marple. The milestone dates from when the canal was first built, and is made of the same stone as the banks. The canal bends to the left, and the curious

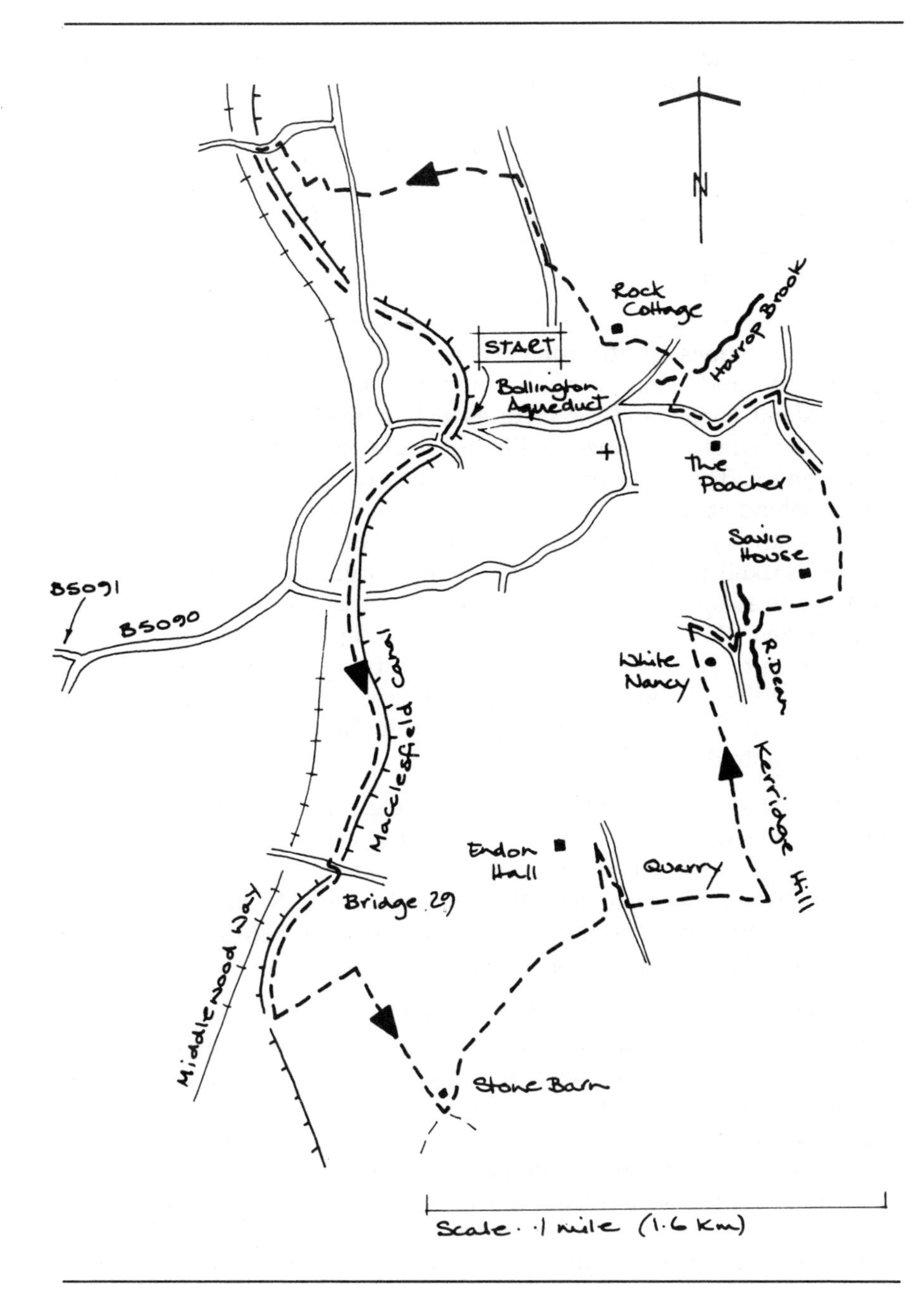
N
Rock Cottage
Harrop Brook
START
Bollington Aqueduct
The Poacher
Savio House
B5091
B5090
White Nancy
R. Dean
Macclesfield Canal
Kerridge Hill
Endon Hall
Quarry
Bridge 29
Middlewood Way
Stone Barn
Scale · 1 mile (1.6 Km)

turrets of Adelphi Mill emerge. It was built in the second half of the 19th century by George Swindells for the benefit of his two sons. The canal was built to transport cotton and silk. After World War Two, rayon and nylon were produced, but the mill was finally closed in the 1970s, although it is currently being restored. The mill's use of water transport was short-lived, however, since in 1869 the Macclesfield - Stockport railway was built alongside the mill. Interestingly enough, that line is now disused, while the canal continues to thrive.

After the next bridge, there is a stone cover for stop planks used to block off sections of the canal. The canal curves around into open countryside and, straight ahead, one can see the higher sections of Macclesfield Forest, and the picturesquely-named Tegg's Nose Country Park, near where the River Bollin rises. On the right, the land slopes away gently. The canal passes a small boatyard on the opposite bank, while behind it are the tree-lined slopes of Kerridge Hill, and White Nancy's strange, white conical monument, believed to have been built by the Gaskell family in memory of the Battle of Waterloo. The next bridge (29) is spectacular, and was designed to take horses across the canal when the towpath changed side. This explains the curious appearance of two sweeping walls, one curving up, the other curving down. Just like the horses, we have to change sides. Follow the path up the bridge, with its stone sets to prevent the horses from slipping, and go round onto the other towpath.

For a short stretch, the canal is in a cutting. This provides shelter for much of the wildlife to be found along the canal banks. It cannot be much fun mooring a boat along this stretch as there is a thick bank of reeds between the canal and the towpath. Birds living in the reeds include bunting and warblers. The canal gradually becomes wider and more open. About 200 yards after the bridge, there is another milestone.

There are industrial buildings further along the canal. The next bridge appears to be little more than an arch, with the majority of its superstructure removed. Take the path up the left hand side of the bridge. At the top, there is a stile on the left hand side. Cross over, and follow the path towards the next stile across a field. After this stile, follow the path which, although not particularly clear, runs fairly straight. If it becomes overgrown, two large oaks dead ahead provide a useful reference point. Go between the two, follow a line of oaks, on the right, and, almost immediately after the first one, the path appears to fork. Take the right fork, crossing over a small ditch, then a stile. On the right hand side, there is a small pond. The path follows the side of the pond, then takes a line across the field to the opposite side, where there is a very small, stone stile, set into a dry stone wall. In the next field, the path follows the right hand edge up a steepish incline.

Cross over a more modern stile, and on the left there is another small pond. Follow the path as it curves round to the left, and head for a stone barn. To the left of the barn, there is a stile and a path leading off into the next field. Take the path around the perimeter of the field on the left hand side. Although it is not that easy to follow, veer into the middle of the field and aim for a stile on the opposite side. Cross this, and follow the path bearing gradually right across the field. It crosses a well-made track, and winds slightly to the left. On the right is Swanscoe Hall, set up on a wooded knoll.

The path comes up to an interesting stile made of three stone flags, in the shape of an arrow head. Follow the field along the right hand edge up a slight incline. On the left is Endon Hall, with its white belvedere in the garden. Straight ahead are the wooded slopes of Kerridge Hill. Cross the stile, and follow the track running along an embankment. Just beyond the stile the path forks, take the fork curving upwards between two dry stone walls. The path is overshadowed on the right by large trees. After a white iron gate, the path is narrower on the left, and the Cheshire plane spreads out, full of leafy villages and gently rolling countryside. Within a hundred yards, the path is overhung by trees on both sides, and comes into a clearing. From here, it doubles back around a sharp bend to the right, and goes uphill to meet the road.

Cross the road and take the footpath leading up from the opposite side. It is a steep track leading to Endon Quarry. Before the entrance to the quarry, take the path branching off to the right. Some shallow steps lead uphill and then the path comes out at a stile. On the other side, there is a small path that goes up to the top of the ridge along Kerridge Hill. The top is marked by a dry stone wall, from here, there are superb views on both sides. Turn round and there is Alderley Edge and the radio telescopes of Jodrell Bank while, to the left, is Macclesfield. In the opposite direction, one can see Manchester, when it is not shrouded by mist or cloud. At the stone wall, turn left, and follow the path.

On the opposite side of the ridge, is the pretty countryside around

Rainow, in the gently rolling hills where the River Dean rises. The ridge path climbs and falls along a switchback course heading almost due north. There is a bird's eye view of Bollington on the left hand side, which reveals how the canal winds its way around the small town. Keep following the wall through a more thickly wooded stretch. The land drops away very steeply to the left, where there are some smallish rock faces at the northern end of the quarry. The path leads up to the monument of White Nancy, and here a view across the whole of Bollington opens up.

There is a steep path down, following the fence beside the monument. At the bottom, there is a well defined track. Turn right, over a cattle grid, and follow the track until it comes to a junction. Take the left hand fork, which winds downhill. On the left is the square chimney of an old mill. Follow the track round and over another cattle grid. The last time I visited here, the trees were full of jays. The track bends round left, and joins another. Keep bearing left, and follow the new track for fifty yards, to a stile on the right hand side.

Cross the stile, and follow a dry stone wall. Within 30 yards, there is a small bridge over the narrow River Dean. On the other side, the path rises steeply, and curves gradually to the left. The path gets narrower as it gets steeper, and there is a dry stone wall on the left. Follow a flight of steps set into the path, through a stile. There are farm buildings belonging to Savio House behind the wall. Cross a wooden stile. Beyond the farm buildings, there is another stile, then a path leading off to the left. After about 500 yards, this comes out on a narrow road. Follow this until it joins a wider road at a T junction. Turn left, and head down the hill, past a good pub, called 'The Poacher', which serves Marston's beers and bar snacks. About a hundred yards futher on, take the path leading off to the right, beside an extraordinary group of pigeon lofts.

A narrow bridge leads over Harrop Brook. Follow the path across a small meadow to a large oak, where there is a gate. The path works its way uphill, and is very overgrown. It comes out into a clearing with houses, and a road. Cross the road, and follow Beeston Rise for a hundred yards to where a gravel track rises steeply straight ahead. Follow the track up hill, past Rock Cottage, as it curves to the left, becoming progressively narrower. Between two steep walls, the path leads up to a wider track. Turn right, and about fifteen yards later, there is a stile on the left. Over the stile, there is a good view of Nab Head, the hill above the picturesque village of Pott Shrigley.

Follow the path to the end of the field where there is another stile. Cross over, and take a diagonal path, slightly to the left across the next field. This leads to a stile onto a road. Turn right on to the road, until the first stile to the left. On the other side, follow the path as it goes downhill across a field, and then follow it between high overgrown hedges. At the bottom, the path gets rather boggy, it then runs along a fence, on the left, up to a stile. Cross the stile, and follow a holly hedge; on the right, cross another stile and the path runs beside a pretty cottage. The path comes out by a gate, onto a drive. After about 200 yards, there is a road, and a cattle grid leads onto it. Turn right and follow the road slightly uphill for a short distance to a footpath leading off left.

Cross the stile here, and follow the path along the right hand edge of the field, around a corner to a small stile leading off along a tree-lined, narrow path. At the end, the path comes out at another gravel track. This track runs for a hundred yards and leads out to a road, by way of a white gate. Turn left, and it is about thirty yards to a bridge (25) over the Macclesfield Canal. Cross the bridge, and take a flight of stone steps down the left hand side to the towpath.

Follow the towpath away from the bridge, past one of the canal's milestones. In the hedge, to the right, I have seen goldfinches and bunting. Go under another bridge (26), which has interesting stonework, largely due to the fact that it crosses the canal at an angle. On the opposite bank, there is Clarence Mill (see photograph on next page), built in the 1820s, and contemporary with the canal. It was constructed for the Swindells family (as with Adelphi Mill) and it was the first Bollington mill to be designed to use water transport. Raw cotton and coal were brought into the wharves, the latter for the mill's great steam engines called 'Perserverance' and 'Success'. The mill was last fully operational in the 1890s, providing high quality cotton for clothing, table linen, and Nottingham lace. It eventually closed in the 1960s.

The towpath crosses Bollington Aqueduct again, and there is the path again leading down to the steep stone steps on the right. It is easy to find the path, since it is directly opposite the timber yard.

The Clarence Mill, Bollington

WALK 29: MACCLESFIELD

Waterway: Macclesfield Canal

Distance: 5 miles

Start: Hurdsfield, where the A5002 crosses the canal. Map reference: 931/744

Map: OS Pathfinder 759

How to get there: It is about a mile from the centre of Macclesfield to where the A5002 road towards Rainow crosses the canal at Hurdsfield. Macclesfield is easily accessible by bus, coach and train.

This walk is only about five miles long, but it includes views across the historic silk town of Macclesfield, the Cheshire Plain, and the former royal hunting grounds of Macclesfield Forest. Although the canal towpaths are some of the best-kept in the area, the section of the walk that leaves the canal can get rather muddy, so strong shoes or boots are recommended.

The Walk:

Start the walk from Hurdsfield, by Chapel-en-le Frith Bridge (34) on the Macclesfield Canal. It is about a mile out of the centre of Macclesfield, along the A5002 towards Rainow and Whaley Bridge. Just before the bridge is the Britannia pub, which sells Greenall Whitley's beer. Cross the bridge, and join the towpath on the far side, heading to the right.

Follow the towpath south towards Macclesfield. The town itself is best reached from Buxton Road Bridge (37). With its different levels, and steep steps, Macclesfield is well worth a detour. The town was first granted a charter in 1261. The parish church of St Michael is an imposing sight, at the top of 108 steps, but although the church was consecrated in 1278, today there is little evidence of its medieval past. The original church was replaced in the 1730s, and this in turn was replaced by the current structure, designed by Bloomfield, at the turn of the century.

Macclesfield is best known as a silk town. The first silk mill was built in

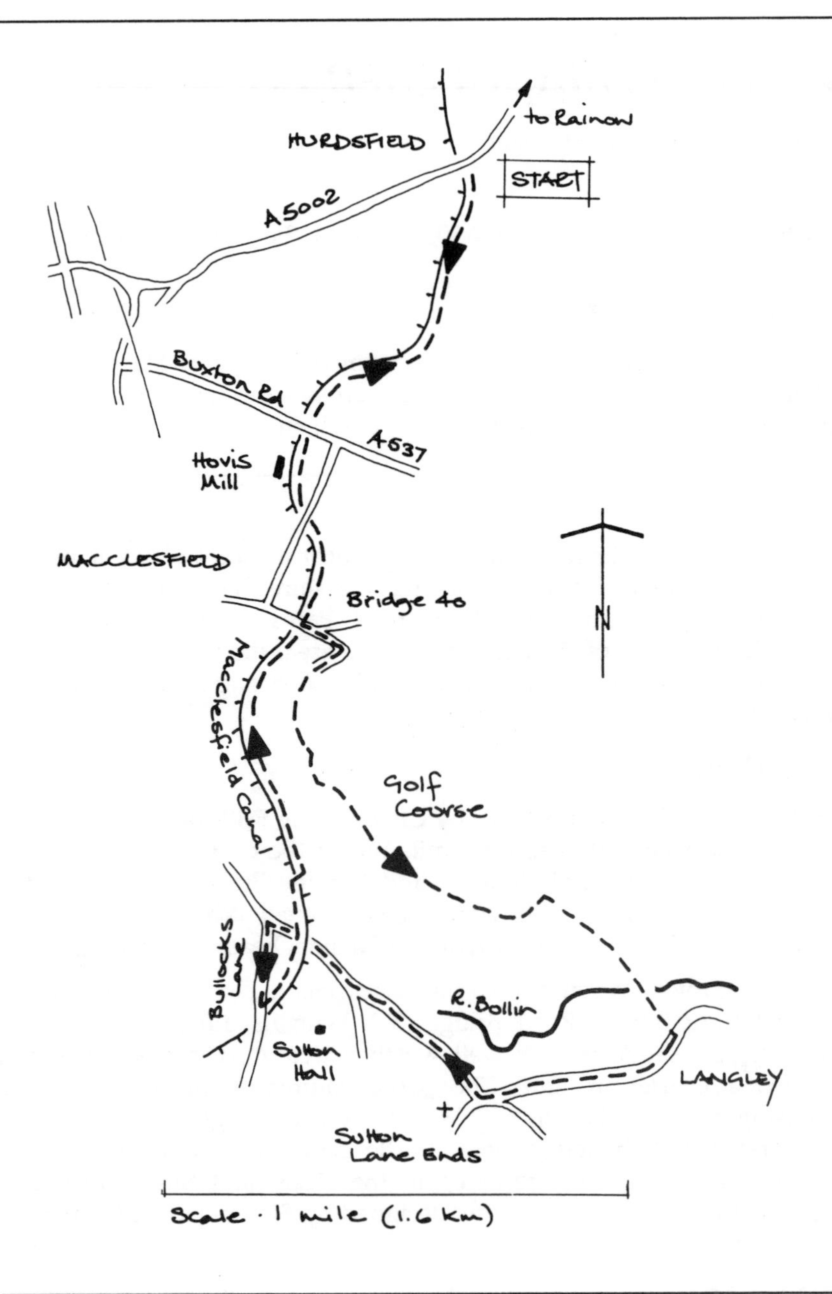
to Rainow
HURDSFIELD
START
A5002
Buxton Rd
A537
Hovis Mill
MACCLESFIELD
Bridge 40
N
Macclesfield Canal
Golf Course
Bullocks Lane
R. Bollin
Sutton Hall
LANGLEY
Sutton Lane Ends
Scale · 1 mile (1.6 km)

1743. Today, it is possible to gain a fascinating insight into the industry at the Silk Museum in Roe Street, and at the Paradise Mill, which was built in the mid 19th century, and has working Jacquard handlooms. The last handloom business finally came to a close as recently as 1980.

After bridge 37 is the former Hovis Mill (Hovis bread was first produced in Macclesfield), and Swettenham Wharf, which is usually busy with pleasure craft. From here, the canal passes under several bridges in fairly quick succession. At Leadbeaters Bridge (40), leave the towpath, and turn left into the road. Follow the right hand fork that leads towards Macclesfield Golf Club. The road becomes a well-made track, and winds around to the right past the clubhouse. Shortly after, there is a stile leading off to the left. Cross over, and follow a good path around the edge of the golf course.

Straight ahead is Tegg's Nose Country Park, and Macclesfield Forest, which was created by the Earls of Chester in the 13th century, and where the Plantagenet kings used to hunt. The last wolf to be found in Britain was killed in the forest. To the left is the canal, and views across the Cheshire Plain to Jodrell Bank and beyond.

The path curves round gradually to the right. Just under a mile after the clubhouse, there is a footpath sign pointing to the right. Follow this and take the path downhill to a stile. This leads further down to a footbridge over the River Bollin, not far from its source in Macclesfield Forest. The footpath comes out at a small road, with the village of Langley to the left. Turn right, and follow the road into Sutton Lane Ends. The village was where the wildlife painter, Charles Tunnicliffe went to school.

After about half a mile, take the first road to the right, and follow it down to the canal aqueduct. Close by is a house where the young James Brindley once lived. Follow the road under the aqueduct, and take the first left into Leek Old Road. The road crosses the Bollin, and rises to climb the canal. Before crossing the bridge (44), join the towpath, and turn left away from the bridge. Down on the opposite side of the canal is the 17th century Sutton Hall, with its chapel which once served as a sanctuary for Catholics.

The towpath crosses Sutton aqueduct, and shortly after on one of the canal's many mileposts, it changes sides at Foden Bank Bridge (43). Follow the towpath on the right hand side of the canal. From here, it is about two miles back to Hurdsfield and the start of the walk.

WALK 30: GAWSWORTH

Waterway: Macclesfield Canal

Distance: Under 5 miles

Start: Oakgrove. Map reference: 917/694

Map: OS Pathfinder 776

How to get there: Oakgrove is two miles south of Macclesfield on the A523 towards Leek. By bus from Macclesfield, take the 201 Derby service.

This is is a pretty walk. It is under five miles, but can and should be extended by having a closer look at Gawsworth. The only tricky part of the walk involves following a rather faint path back to the canal. Otherwise, it is very straightforward - and takes in one of Cheshire's finest manor houses, and a fine stretch of canal.

Start the walk at Oakgrove. About two miles south of Macclesfield on the A523 towards Leek, there is a crossroads and the road off to the west crosses the Macclesfield Canal which runs close to the right hand side road at this point. It is possible to park on the road leading to the left at the crossroads.

The Walk:

Cross Royal Oak Swing Bridge (49), and join the towpath, heading away from the bridge to the right. A few hundred yards from the bridge, there is one of the many mileposts that one finds on the Macclesfield canal, reading Marple 14 miles and on the reverse Hall Green 12 miles. Just beyond, there is a set of steps. Follow them down to path which is invariably rather muddy.

It is a short distance to where the path crosses a narrow stream that runs south into the reservoir at North Rode, and eventually into the River Dane. On the other side, the path rises across a field in the direction of a farm. The path leads round to the left of the farm to meet the drive leading onto a road. At the road, turn right, and follow it past

Whereton's Farm on the left, and over the Macclesfield - London railway line, languishing in a deep cutting. A quarter of a mile after the railway, there is a farm on the left and, just after, a well-marked path leading off to the left.

Gawsworth Hall

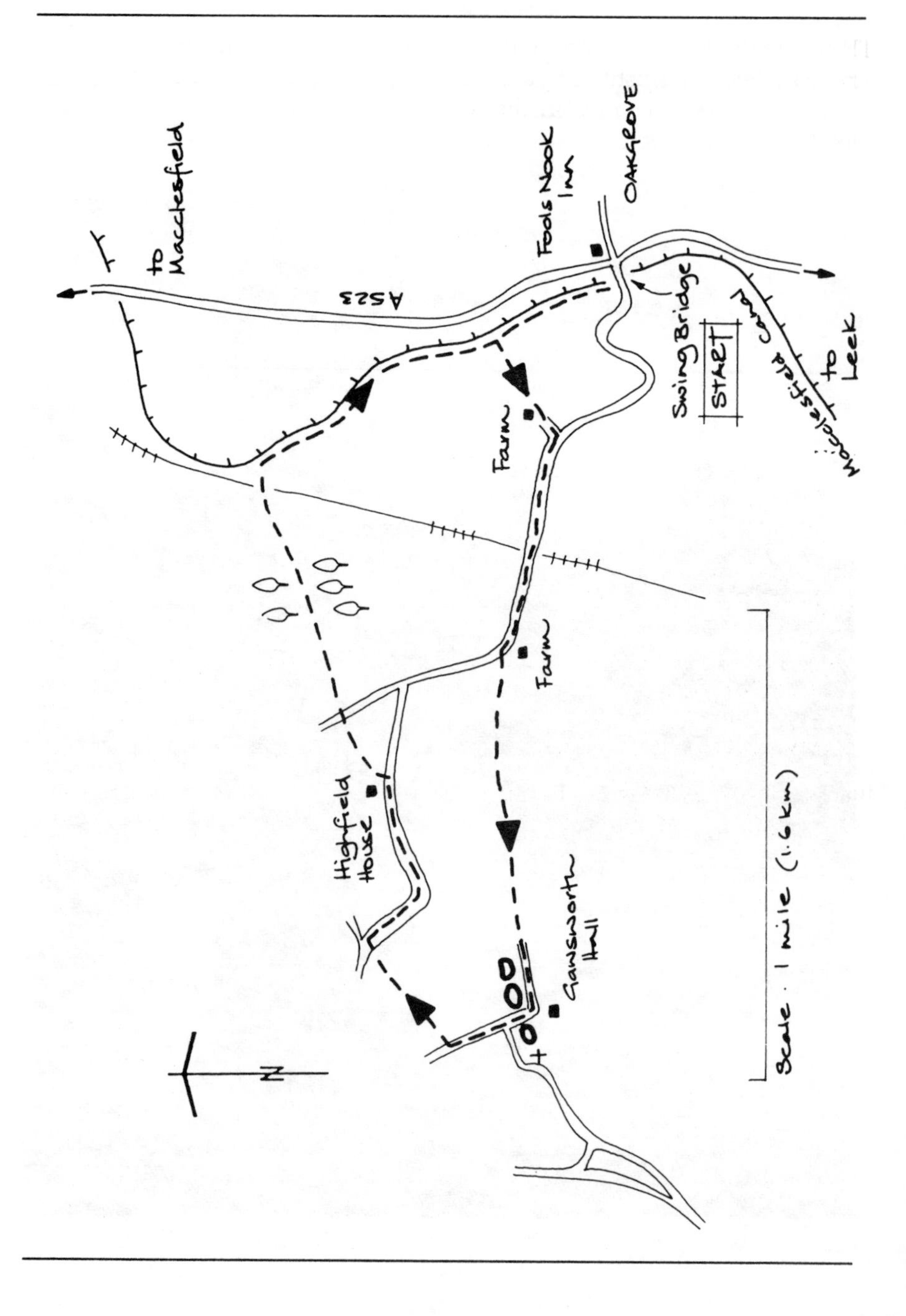
to Macclesfield
A523
Fools Nook Inn
OAKGROVE
Swing Bridge
START
Macclesfield Canal
to Leek
Farm
Farm
Highfield House
Gawsworth Hall
N
Scale: 1 mile (1.6 km)

This path is a well-used route to Gawsworth, and is easy to follow. There are two wooden gates along the path which follows a very straight line in the direction of Gawsworth Hall. A stile takes the path into a field, keep heading straight ahead with the edge of the field on your left. Cross over another stile, and the path becomes a more established track and runs past two ponds on the right. To the left is the front of the hall. Gawsworth Hall is Tudor, with additional work around 1700. The Fitton coat of arms is carved on one side of the building, and the Hall was the home of Mary Fitton, a maid of honour at the Court of Queen Elizabeth I, and thought to be the dark lady of Shakespeare's sonnets. Gawsworth was the home of the Fitton family from 1306 to the late 17th century. The hall has a mile long park which contains the Fitton family's tilting ground.

Follow what is now the drive to the hall as it winds to the right between the second pond and a third one beyond. From this point, there is a view of one of the most picturesque villages in Cheshire with its church slightly raised above one of the ponds and in ascending order the fine architecture of the New Hall, the Old Rectory, and Gawsworth Old Hall. St James, Gawsworth was built between the 15th century and the 16th century, and did not suffer from the interference of any Victorian architects. The Old Rectory is a timber-framed 15th century house, built by Rector Baguley in 1470. The large New Hall was begun in 1707, but never completed.

Just south of Gawsworth is the tomb of Maggoty Johnson, known as Lord Flame, one of the last English jesters. It is said that he returned to Gawsworth, after suffering complete rejection in London, and died in 1773.

Where the drive meets the road, follow it to the right. A few hundred yards further on, there is a footpath sign on the right. Cross over a stile, and follow a well defined path that bears slightly to the left. Less than half a mile further on, it comes out of another road. Turn right, and follow the road. Keep to the right. There are several paths leading off the road, but stay on it until you come across Highfield House on your left. Just beyond it, a footpath leads off to the left. It is not the easiest path to follow, but it is not far from the canal. Follow the edge of the field, working around to the right to a stile on the left hand side. Go over the stile and it is a short distance to where another path crosses. Keep straight ahead, and the path enters Danes Moss Nature Reserve.

It is a little over a quarter of a mile from here to the railway line. Take great care in crossing over, as express trains use it. On the other side, there is a stile. Cross over, and follow the path up to where Broadhurst Swing Bridge (47) goes over the canal. Turn right, and follow the towpath. The canal bends to run close by the main Macclesfield to Leek road, with Sutton Reservoir on the far side of the road, with its dinghies and water sports. It is just under a mile along the towpath back to the Royal Oak Swing Bridge. On the other side of the bridge - a new hydraulically-operated one having recently replaced the notoriously difficult old swing bridge - is Oakgrove, and the Fools Nook Inn which serves good food and Higson's beer.

WALK 31: BOSLEY FLIGHT

Waterway: Macclesfield Canal

Distance: Under 6 miles

Start: Top of the Bosley Flight at North Rode. Map reference: 905/670

Map: OS Pathfinder 776

How to get there: Four miles south of Macclesfield on the A523 towards, turn right towards North Rode to where the road crosses the canal. By bus from Macclesfield, take the 201 service.

This is a gentle walk of under six miles. It shows how the canal and the River Dane weave in and out, and has good views of nineteenth century railway and waterway engineering. Although the whole of the Macclesfield canal towpath is attractive walking country, this is one of the quieter corners - literally a corner where the canal bends from heading south to due west into Congleton. A worthwile visit, while in the area, is Gawsworth Hall three miles north of North Rode. The hall is a 16th century half-timbered manor house, once the home of Mary Fitton, maid of honour at the court of Queen Elizabeth I, and supposed to be the dark lady of Shakespear's sonnets.

Bosley Reservoir is about a mile to the east of the canal, and contains over 400 million gallons of water.

This walk begins at the head of the Bosley flight on the Macclesfield Canal. Heading south on the A523 from Macclesfield to Leek, after about four miles turn right towards North Rode. Within a mile the road crosses the canal, and it is possible to park on the right hand side of the road just before the bridge. To the left, there is lock one of the twelve that make up the Bosley flight. These twelve drop the canal by 118 feet within a mile, and were planned by Thomas Telford, with his preference for grouping locks in flights. Unlike many narrow canals, these locks have sets of double gates at both ends, and the Bosley locks are the only locks on the canal (with the exception of Hall Green Stop Lock).

The Walk:

Cross the bridge (54), and take the path down to the towpath. This brings one out by the lock keeper's cottage and the long, stepped pound beside it, which was once used to help save water when a lot of boats came down the flight. Head downhill from the lock, under the bridge, along the broad, well-kept towpath. On the left are the rolling hills of the southern end of the Pennines. It is not far to the next lock, and directly beyond it in the distance are the steep slopes of 'The Cloud'. To the right of the lock, a wide overflow drains the canal into a pool on the right of the towpath. The next two locks follow in quick succession and are of a similar design. The locks are made of gritstone.

Lock 5 is just before the A54 Buxton to Congleton road bridge. To the other side is lock 6, and there is a short pound between it and lock 7. The pound between locks 7 and 8 is shorter still, and on the opposite bank there is a thick weed bed, no doubt home for roach, dace and perch. Immediately after lock 8 is a stone built bridge. The pounds between locks continue to be short, and some of them are almost as wide as they are long, deliberately broad to contain as much water as possible. In fact the pound between locks 10 and 11 appears to go off into a backwater on the opposite side. On the left, along this stretch, are the remains of the Macclesfield to Leek railway.

After lock 11, the pound forms a wide basin, before the old railway bridge crosses it. The canal curves around to lock 12, the last in the flight. Soon after, the canal curves further to the right over the River Dane aqueduct, with its splendid, coloured railings. 'The Cloud' appears to draw ever nearer while, on the right, one can see the magnificent arches of the main Macclesfield to London railway line's viaduct over the River Dane and its broad valley.

A hundred yards after crossing the aqueduct, go up the side of bridge 57 and turn right. Cross a stile and follow a well-defined path between trees with a fence on the left hand side. Do not follow the path that veers off to a field on the left, but keep along the line of the fence. The path gradually curves its way downhill. At the bottom there is a gate with a rather ricketty stile, cross over and follow the path uphill again. To the right, a small brook joins the Dane. The path is still fenced on the left side, and follow it towards the railway viaduct. The wooded valley of the Dane runs parallel to the path on its right hand side. There is an

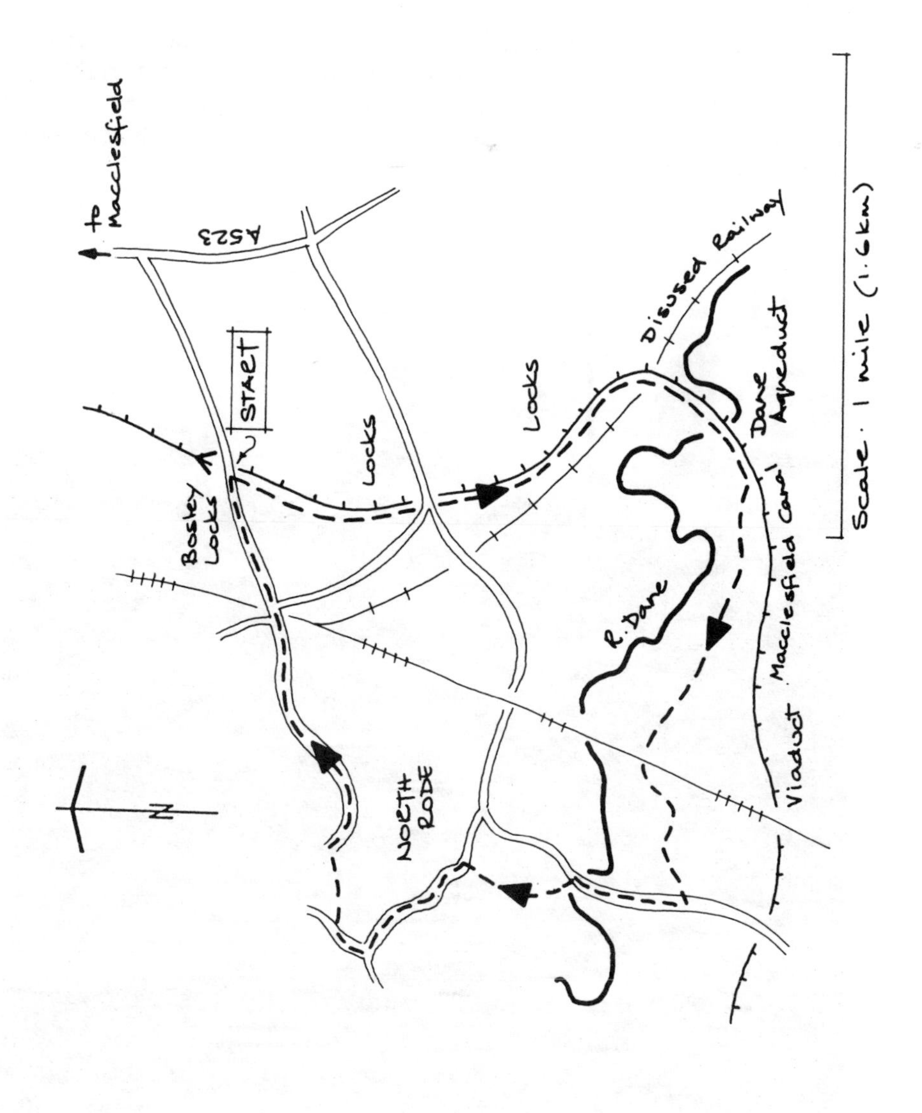
to Macclesfield
A523
START
Locks
Locks
Bosley Locks
Disused Railway
Dane Aqueduct
Macclesfield Canal
R. Dane
Viaduct
NORTH RODE
N
Scale: 1 mile (1.6km)

iron gate into the next field. The path goes under the second left of the viaduct's arches, after passing through another iron gate.

Once under the viaduct, the path curves round gradually to the left, and leads into a rather tatty farmyard. Go through the yard to where a small road leads out of it. Lapwings often hover about here looking for food in the fields. The small road leads up to the busy A54. Turn right, and follow the road carefully as there is no footpath. It is not for long until the road crosses the Dane over an old stone bridge, with the traffic going in single file, one way at a time.

The top of the Bosley Flight

Just after the bridge, there is a stile leading to a path on the left. After following the Dane for 20 yards, the path goes up a steep bank, to the right, and down again to a wooden bridge over a brook joining the river. Follow the edge of the field to a very steep stile. Turn left, and follow the path with a track that joins from the left. Head for a gate in the opposite side of the field. The pretty village of North Rode, with St Michael's, its handsome church, is on the hill to the left. Go through the gate, and turn left up a small road that winds uphill past a large dairy farm with a herd of Friesians. At the top of the hill, turn right into a track, just in front of the nineteenth century church.

After a white wooden gate, there is a well-made track. Fifty yards further on, take the right fork downhill. This leads to a stile. Follow the right hand edge of the next field to another stile. Cross over onto a well-made track. Turn right, and follow the wooded drive that leads from the Manor House. There is a large lake on the left, and the drive passes a round overflow which takes excess water down to the Dane; it also suggests that the lake was man-made. Carry on uphill until the path comes out by a set of gates. Go straight ahead, and cross the Macclesfield to London railway line. Go over the crossroads on the other side, and follow the road back to the canal bridge by Bosley Locks to the start of the walk. Just on the other side is a feeder stream from Bosley Reservoir to keep the flight topped up.

WALK 32: THE CLOUD

Waterway: Macclesfield Canal

Distance: 8 miles

Start: Buglawton, where the A54 crosses the canal. Map reference: 877/638

Map: OS Pathfinder 776

How to get there: the A54 to Buxton crosses the canal about a mile out of Congleton. By bus, take the K80, or K81 Congleton to Leek services.

The walk is about 8 miles, and involves a broad mixture of terrain. Some parts are neglected or rather overgrown, so boots or strong shoes should be worn. Climbing up to The Cloud is moderately strenuous, so this walk is rather more than a Sunday afternoon stroll. The views are very rewarding, however, and the canal passes through some delightful countryside. Parts of the walk are some distance from shelter, so it is wise to take waterproofs. There are few places where refreshments may be bought, so it might be useful to take some food and drink on the walk.

Start the walk at Buglawton, about a mile along the A54, heading out of Congleton towards Buxton. The road crosses the Macclesfield Canal, but the towpath runs along the near side of the bridge (68). Parking is not particularly easy, but the roads leading off to the right, just before the bridge, can be used.

The Walk:

Take the path down to the towpath, and turn right. Follow the towpath for less than a mile, passing under Wallworth's Bridge (69), Galley's Bridge (70), then the railway bridge carrying the main Macclesfield to London line. Bearing in mind how close the canal is, here, to Congleton town centre, it is pleasantly wooded with good views of the Pennines to the east. A number of small brooks run under the canal to feed the River Dane.

Shortly after the railway bridge is bridge 71, a footbridge. Cross the

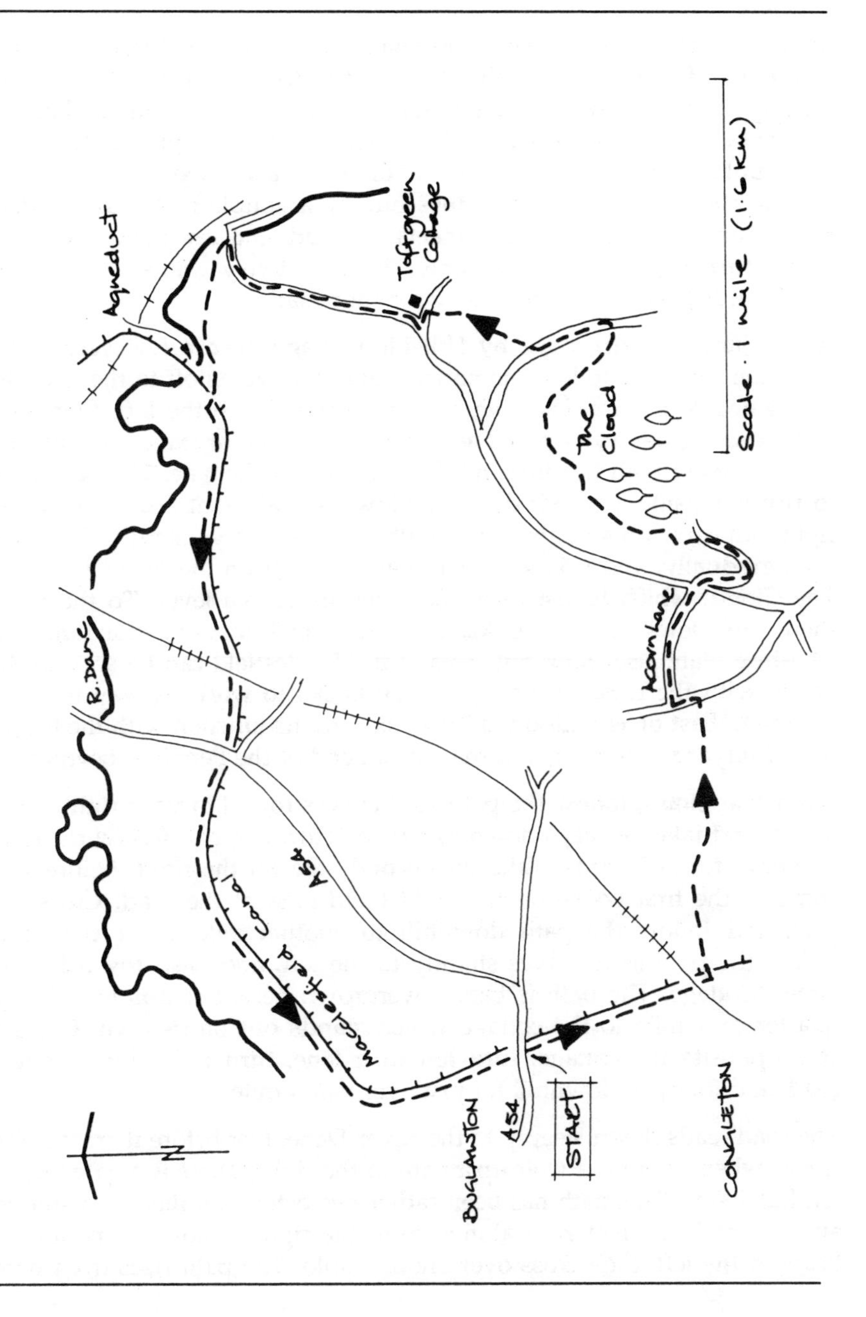
Aqueduct
Toft green Cottage
The Cloud
Scale: 1 mile (1.6 Km)
R. Dane
Acorn Lane
A54
Macclesfield Canal
START
A54
BUGLAWTON
CONGLETON
N

canal here, and follow a well-made path along a wooded stretch, taking care not to follow the path that veers off to the left to run close by the railway line. Follow the path into a meadow; should it become overgrown, keep to the edge of the field, and curve gradually to the right until it becomes a more identifiable track. About a mile after leaving the canal, the track comes out by a couple of houses at Pool Bank. Turn left when the track meets the road, and less than a hundred yards, turn right into Acorn Lane. The attractively walled lane climbs for about half a mile before joining a minor road.

At the junction, turn right by Hillside Cottage, then a few yards later cross the road and follow the narrow lane that winds off to the left. The lane gains height quickly and, after a tight bend to the left, there is a sign pointing the way up to The Cloud. At this point leave the lane and follow a good path heading uphill to the left of the lane. The path rises to run alongside a wood; do not follow the path that heads off to the right, but carry on straight ahead with the wood to your right. The path rises gradually, and it is less than half a mile from the wood to top of The Cloud, which is just over 1000 feet above sea level. To the west, there are views across the Macclesfield Canal to Congleton and the Cheshire plain stretching out beyond it. Macclesfield can be seen to the north, with the canal rising up Bosley Locks to work its way towards the town. East of The Cloud is the Dane, and its junction with the feeder from Rudyard Reservoir, and the bottom end of the Pennines beyond.

From The Cloud, follow the path as it curves round to your right, cross a stile, and take the steps down to a road. Turn left, and follow the road downhill for 200 yards. Take the second stile on the right, before you come to the first house on the right hand side of the road. Cross the stile, and follow the path downhill to another stile. After this stile, follow the path as it curves slightly to the left, and head towards Toft Green Cottage. The path is badly overgrown here, but it is less than a quarter of a mile to the cottage which stands out on its own. Cross a stile opposite the cottage, turn left in a lane, turn right, into a small road, and follow it downhill for just over half a mile.

The road leads down steeply to the River Dane. Just before it crosses the river, (where there is a weir upstream to the right), there is a gate on the left hand side. This path has been rather neglected, but there is a stile to aim for, and the river runs alongside to the right. Follow the path as it bears to the left, then cross over another stile. The path rises from here to another stile. Cross over into a field. From here it is a short distance to the canal. If the line of the path is unclear, aim for the bridge. From the top of Old Driving Lane Bridge (57) there is a good view of the Macclesfield Canal aqueduct across the River Dane.

Cross the bridge to the towpath, and turn left. Follow the towpath under the next two bridges, and then go under the railway line again. Just afterwards, the attractive half timbered Crossley Hall Farm comes into view close to the canal. From here, the River Dane runs parallel with the canal, coming in and out of view over the next two miles. At Stanley's Bridge (65), the canal bends to the left, and heads away from the river, running alongside Havannah, now part of Congleton, but once a village built around a cigar works which went out of business long ago. It is just over half a mile from bridge 65 back to where the A54 crosses the canal at Buglawton.

Canal Notes:

The completion of the Trent and Mersey canal in 1777 led to calls for an alternative route between Manchester, the Potteries and the Midlands. Lobbying and discussions took place for over twenty years and, in 1825, Thomas Telford was asked to examine the possibility of linking the Trent and Mersey to the Peak Forest Canal. It was logical that the canal would pass through the towns of Macclesfield and Congleton, and Telford recommended a 28 mile route from Marple to Kidsgrove. Although the canal was built by William Crossley, many of its features reveal the influence of Telford. Primarily, it follows the straightest possible course by way of deep cuttings and grand embankments.

Apart from the flight of 12 locks at Bosley, the only other lock on the canal is the stop lock at Hall Green, where the Macclesfield Canal and the Trent and Mersey meet, which is to ensure that water levels are maintained. The level of the Macclesfield is topped up from Bosley and Sutton reservoirs. Opened in 1831, the Macclesfield is one of the more recent canals. Coming some time after the canal boom, there were even plans to construct a railway along the route, rather than a canal. Despite the subsequent expansion of the railways, the Macclesfield Canal thrived. Most of the trade upon the canal was coal and cotton, and the Macclesfield Canal remained busy longer than some of its neighbours. By the end of the 19th century, trade had declined, and nowadays it is only used by tourists, as it forms part of the 'Cheshire Ring'.

WALK 33: LITTLE MORETON HALL

Waterway: Macclesfield Canal

Distance: $5^1/_2$ miles

Start: Bleeding Wolf, Hall Green. Map reference: 833/562

Map: OS Pathfinder 792

How to get there: From Congleton, it is six miles south of Congleton on the A34 to the Bleeding Wolf. By bus from Congleton, take the 315 or 94 services.

This walk is about five and half miles long. It passes three of Cheshire's most unusual large houses. Ramsdell Hall, Little Moreton Hall and Rode Hall are very different, and give a good indication of the diversity

Little Moreton Hall

of large scale domestic architecture to be found in Cheshire. The countryside is lush and rural, and it is difficult to imagine that less than five miles to the south, are Kidsgrove and then the Potteries. Along the canal, there are several places where refreshments may be bought, and at Kent Green, there is a canalside shop where as well as food, guidebooks and souvenirs can be bought.

The Walk:

Start the walk from the Bleeding Wolf at Hall Green. The pub, which serves food, is on the A34, about six miles south of Congleton, just after Scholar Green. A little beyond the pub, turn right, and follow the road up to bridge 94, and join the towpath on the nearside, heading left, away from the bridge. It is a short distance to Hall Green Lock, which rises just one foot, and is the division between the Trent and Mersey Canal, and the Macclesfield Canal to the north.

Follow the towpath as the canal runs parallel with the main Macclesfield to London railway line in a cutting on the right. Beyond, the ridge which is dominated by Mow Cop is impossible to miss. The path passes Kent Green, on the left, and the charming Bird in Hand pub. After Kent Green Bridge (87), the canal passes Ramsdell Hall on the right, and a Macclesfield Canal milepost. The unusual Ramsdell Hall has two entrances, and was built in the mid eighteenth century. Less than a quarter of mile after Ramsdell Hall is Rowndes No. 2 bridge (86).

Just before the bridge take the footpath leading off, and follow the signs for Little Moreton Hall. The path joins a well made track for some of the way, and runs alongside a hedge. The path bears slightly to the right. Cross over two stiles and, after the second one, turn left, and head in the direction of Little Moreton Hall. The path comes up to another stile. Cross over onto a track, and head along it with the Hall to your right.

Little Moreton Hall was built between 1559 and 1589 (although the Great Hall dates back to the late 15th century) by the Moreton family, and is partly defended by a moat. It is a bizarre building and the 75′ by 12′6″ hung gallery running along the top storey makes it look particularly precarious, as if a strong wind would blow the lot down. For all of its eccentricities, Little Moreton Hall has a strong claim to being one of the finest English black and white houses. Inside, there is a priest's hole, and fine examples of Elizabethan plasterwork. There is also a chapel, and a courtyard.

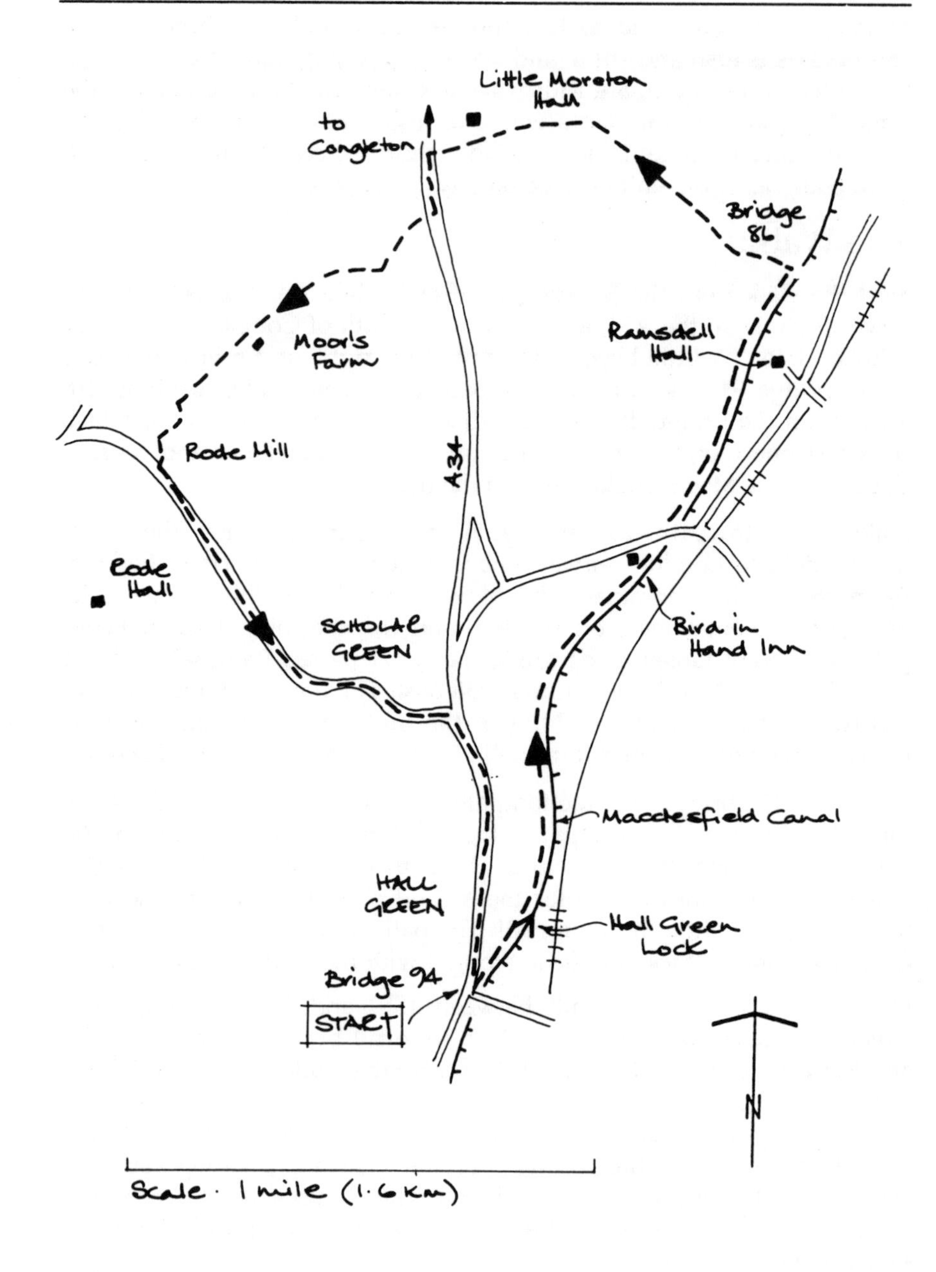
Little Moreton Hall
to Congleton
Bridge 86
Ramsdell Hall
Moor's Farm
Rode Mill
A34
Rode Hall
SCHOLAR GREEN
Bird in Hand Inn
Macclesfield Canal
HALL GREEN
Hall Green Lock
Bridge 94
START
N
Scale · 1 mile (1·6 km)

It is a couple of hundred yards from the hall to the A34. At the road, turn right for 200 yards, to a footpath on the right hand side of the road. Cross the stile, and follow the left hand edge of the field to the next stile. The land rises and follow the path with the farm on your right, to where it meets a track. Turn right and follow the footpath sign. The path is clearly marked, and leads round to the right hand side of Moor's Farm. It joins a well made track. Follow this to where it joins a road beside Rode Mill, which is by a stream which goes on to form the River Wheelock. Heading right along the road, one can glimpse Rode Pool through the trees. For the purpose of this walk, however, turn left, and follow the road past the entrance to Rode Hall. It is about a mile from Rode Mill to the A34.

Rode Hall was originally built in early 18th century with subsequent additions once the estate had come into the hands of the Wilbraham family. In the 19th century what now appears to be the main body of the house was built onto the side. The man responsible for the folly at Mow Cop, Randle Wilbraham clearly oversaw the evolution of Rode Hall from what now appears to be fairly humble origins.

At the main road, turn right, and it is about a half a mile to the Bleeding Wolf at Hall Green, and the start of the walk.

WALK 34: MOW COP

Waterway: Macclesfield Canal

Distance: 6 miles

Start: Acker's Crossing. Map reference: 848/589

Map: OS Pathfinder 792

How to get there: From Congleton, head south on the A34 for five miles to Scholar Green, then turn left and follow the road over the canal to the start of the walk. By bus from Congleton, take the 94, or 315 services.

This walk is six miles long, and it involves some fairly arduous upping and downing. Strong shoes, and a compass are recommended. Mow Cop is one of the furthest points, to the south east of the River Mersey's catchment area, and the streams that rise on its slopes form the River Wheelock, a tributary of the River Dane which in turn joins the Weaver. The rock on which the village sits (properly, Yoredale Rocks) is the oldest in Cheshire. I prefer to walk the route anti-clockwise, with the ascent to the top coming after the towpath walk. If the walk is carried out clockwise, it is very hard to resist the charms of Kent Green's canalside pubs, having climbed Mow Cop, and with only a couple of miles of flat path to go back to Acker's Crossing. For fans of the Macclesfield Canal, it is well worth extending the walk by following the towpath after bridge 89 for the extra two miles that lead beyond the lock at Hall Green to Red Bull Aqueduct, where the canal crosses the Trent and Mersey, only to join it a short distance further on at Harding's Wood Junction.

Start the walk at Acker's Crossing on the Macclesfield Canal. Heading south on the A34 from Congleton it is about 5 miles to Scholar Green. Take the second left, after Little Moreton Hall, and follow the road for 2 miles, over the canal, past Ramsdell Hall on the left, to where the road crosses the canal for a second time. This is Acker's Crossing, where there are plenty of places to park.

The Walk:

Cross the bridge (85), and join the towpath, heading away from the bridge to the left. On the right, the land rises steeply, with Mow Cop the hightest point along the ridge. After just over half a mile, a path crosses bridge 86, and to the right, leads off to Little Moreton Hall. Shortly after there is a good view of Ramsdell Hall on the opposite side of the canal. One of the Macclesfield's mileposts, a few hundred yards after the hall, reads Hall Green $4^1/_2$ miles, Marple 25 miles.

The canal runs through attractive countryside and, after bridge 87, Kent Green is on the left. Famous for its pubs, Kent Green and the Bird in Hand in particular, attract many real ale enthusiasts. Follow the canal as far as Morris Bridge (89), and cross over to the other side. Head along the path to the tunnel under the Macclesfield to London railway line. On the other side, cross a stile and follow a good path bearing slightly to the right towards another stile. Beyond is a wood and a path joins from the right. Keep going straight ahead, and a little further on be sure not to follow the path leading off to the left. After the wood, the path rises gradually up to a footbridge and a stile. Keep on in a straight line, as the path beyond the stile is not that well defined. A road comes into view. Follow the path round to the left for a short distance to where it joins the road by a stile. Cross over and turn left. Head uphill along the road for just over a quarter of a mile to a - junction. Follow this road up into the pretty village of Mow Cop.

It is just over half a mile to where the road diverges. Keep to the right, and head uphill for a quarter of a mile to the square towered St Thomas's church. At the church, turn left, and follow the steep, narrow road that bears right to the Old Man of Mow at the top. From this superb vantage point, over 1000 feet above sea level, the entire Cheshire plain opens out to the north and west. The canal can be seen clearly and its junction with the Trent and Mersey. To the South, there is a view across Stoke-on-Trent and the Potteries.

Mow Cop, meaning Bald Hill, is built around Mow Cop Castle. It is in actual fact, a folly, being no more than a fake ruin. Built in 1754, by Randle Wilbraham, it is and always has been just a large tower with an arch. At one time, the top of Mow Cop had one of the beacons originally built to warn of the Spanish Armada. It was on the summit of Mow Cop where the Primitive Methodists held their very first meeting.

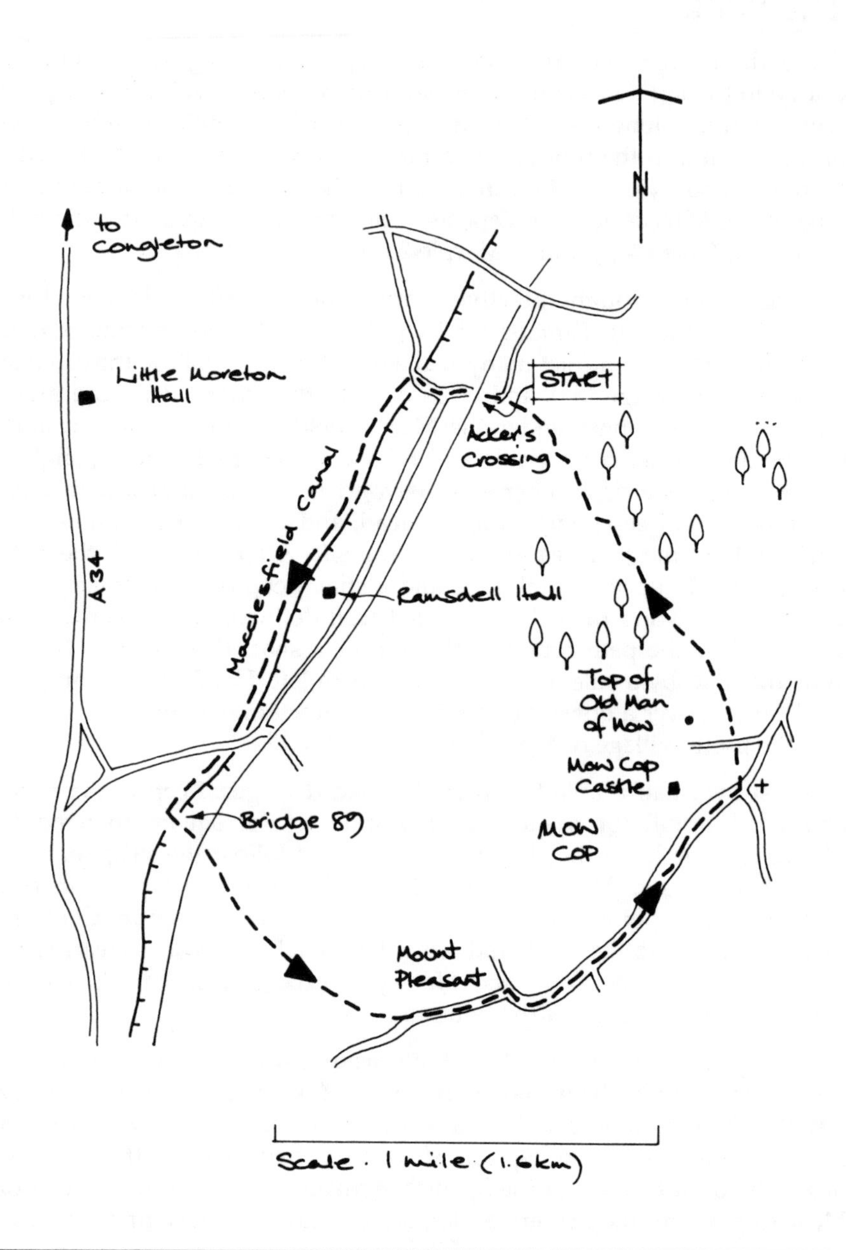
N
to Congleton
Little Moreton Hall
START
Acker's Crossing
Macclesfield Canal
A34
Ramsdell Hall
Top of Old Man of Mow
Mow Cop Castle
Bridge 89
MOW COP
Mount Pleasant
Scale · 1 mile (1.6km)

From the Old Man of Mow, take the path down the hill away from the village. After a stile, the path leads through some particularly pretty woodland. It is a good, clearly marked path that drops steeply through the wood for over a mile. After the woodland, it is less than half a mile before the path becomes a well made track. This leads to the railway line, and to Acker's Crossing on the other side. From here, it is a short walk to the bridge (85) over the canal and the start of the walk.

WALK 35: RED BULL JUNCTION

Waterways: Macclesfield and Trent and Mersey Canals

Distance: 6 miles

Start: Rising Sun, Kent Green. Map reference: 838/575

Map: OS Pathfinder 792

How to get there: Five miles out of Congleton on the A34, turn left at Scholar Green to where the road crosses the canal at Kent Green. By bus from Congleton, take the 315 or 94 services.

This walk is six miles long, and does not involve any great effort. It includes the splendid aqueduct, locks and junction of the Macclesfield and Trent and Mersey Canals and provides an interesting contrast between the more rural former and the more commercial latter with its double locks to speed up traffic. From the junction, the Trent and Mersey drops dramatically to cross the Cheshire plain, before joining up with the Bridgewater Canal at Preston Brook.

Start the walk from the Rising Sun Inn at Kent Green. Heading south on the A34 from Congleton, it is about five miles to Scholar Green. Take the second right after Little Moreton Hall, and follow the road for a mile to where it crosses the Macclesfield Canal. It is possible to park close to the canal bridge.

The Walk:

The towpath is on the near side. Turn right, heading away from the bridge. Pass bridge 88, and the delightful Bird in Hand Inn. It is about a mile to Hall Green Lock, where a rise of only 1 foot separates the water of the Macclesfield Canal from that of the Trent and Mersey.

After the thick woodland around Hall Green, it is about a mile to Red Bull aqueduct. Here the Macclesfield Canal crosses the Trent and Mersey prior to joining it just over half a mile further on. At bridge 98, cross over, and follow the path down to the lock at the junction of the two canals. Cross the lock, and turn left.

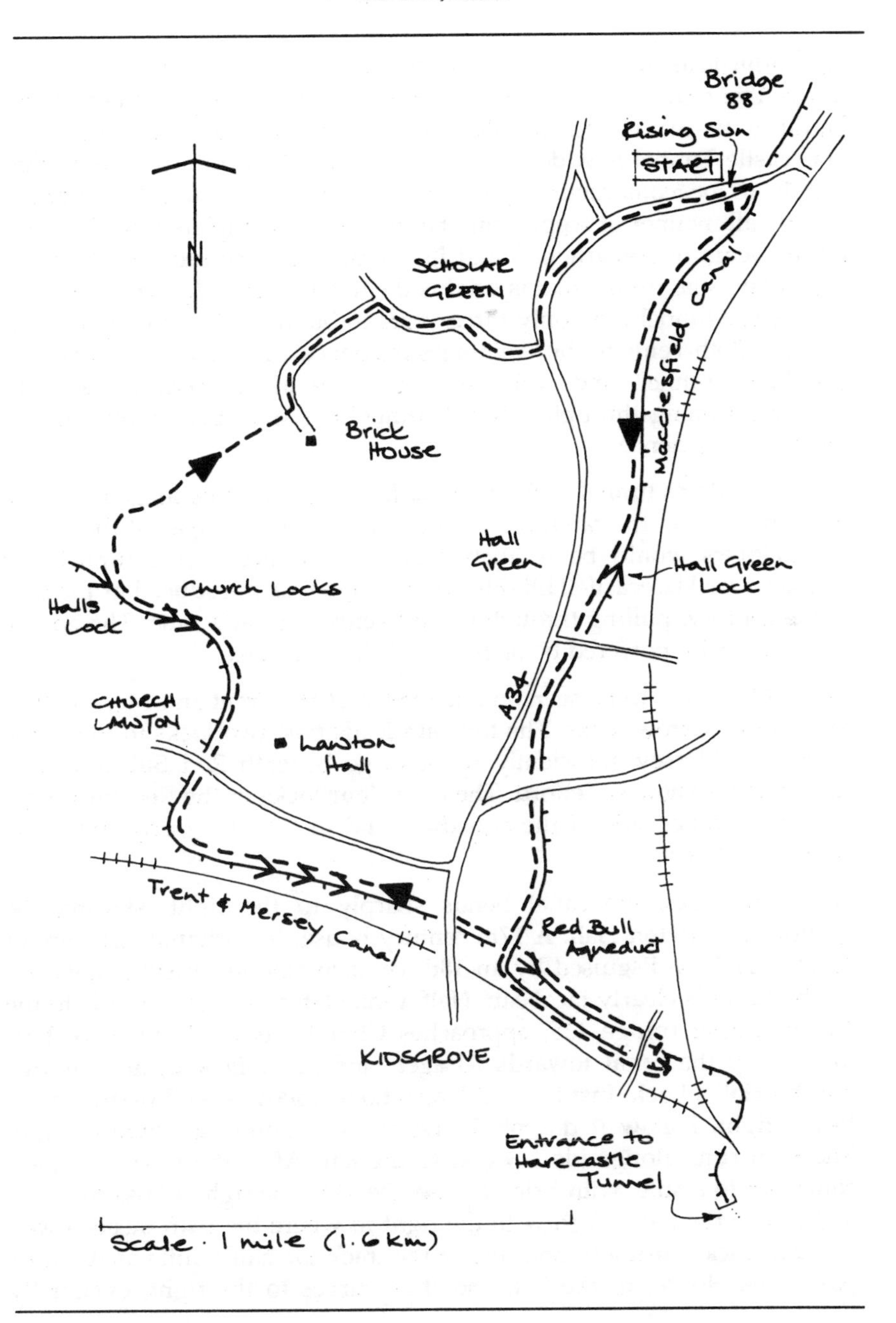
Bridge 88
Rising Sun
START
N
SCHOLAR GREEN
Brick House
Macclesfield Canal
Hall Green
Hall Green Lock
Church Locks
Halls Lock
CHURCH LAWTON
Lawton Hall
A34
Trent & Mersey Canal
Red Bull Aqueduct
KIDSGROVE
Entrance to Harecastle Tunnel
Scale · 1 mile (1.6km)

For enthusiasts, it is well worth turning right, when joining the towpath at the Trent and Mersey Canal, as it is less than a mile to the northern entrance to the Harecastle Tunnel. It is of particular importance as Harecastle Tunnel is widely thought to be the first tunnel of more than a mile to be constructed anywhere in the world. Built by Brindley, despite all manner of scepticism, the tunnel was completed in 1777, after eleven years of construction and its entrance can be seen on the right. Nowadays, the tunnel that is used is the one by Telford, opened in 1827. The newer tunnel took only three years to build. Both were operational into the 20th century, but mining subsidence caused great damage to Brindley's tunnel, and sadly it had to be abandoned. In fact, the towpath running through Telford's tunnel has since been removed as a result of subsidence.

Since Brindley's tunnel had no towpath, boats had to be legged through by men lying on the cabin roof and pushing their feet against the tunnel roof. Horses would be unhitched at the entrance to the tunnel and walked over Harecastle Hill. Electric haulage was introduced at the turn of the century, pulling through up to twenty craft at a time. The advent of individually powered boats rendered this obsolete.

Like all the locks to be seen on this stretch of the Trent and Mersey, they are double narrow locks. The towpath leads past two locks to lower the Trent and Mersey sufficiently for it to go beneath Red Bull aqueduct designed by Thomas Telford. The other four locks in the Red Bull flight are on the other side of the aqueduct, and in total they drop the canal by nearly 55 feet.

After the locks, the canal bends sharply to the right, skirting the grounds of Lawton Hall. A 17th century house, the original structure of Lawton Hall is disguised by an 18th century exterior. Inside, however, the building is clearly Jacobean. Half a mile later, the canal bends to the left and, after bridge 135, approaches Church Locks. These two deep locks drop the canal towards Alsager, and are followed, after bridge 136, by Hall's Lock. Just beyond Hall's Lock, follow a well marked path to the right. Follow it downhill, and cross a footbridge bearing right. The path runs along side a wood to the left. After the wood the path comes up to a stile, with Brick House ahead to the right. Cross the stile, and follow the path, slightly to the right to where the path meets a well defined track. Turn left, and follow the track for half a mile as it winds past Brick House, to the left, and then curves to the right, eventually coming out at a road. Turn right, and it is about half a mile to the A34 and Scholar Green.

Turn left for a few hundred yards, and the turning to Kent Green and the start of the walk is on the right. Follow the road for about a mile back to the Rising Sun Inn and the Macclesfield Canal.

BIBLIOGRAPHY

The Bridgewater Canal Handbook, Copyright of The Manchester Ship Canal Company

J. Corbridge, *A Pictorial History of the Mersey and Irwell Navigation,* E. J. Morten, 1979

R. Freethy, *The River Mersey,* Terence Dalton Limited, 1985

C. Hadfield and G. Biddle, *The Canals of North West England Volumes 1 and 2,* David and Charles, 1970

Nicholson/*Ordnance Survey Guide to the Waterways 3: North, 4th edition,* Ordnance Survey, 1989

D. Owen, *Canals to Manchester,* Manchester University Press, 1977

N. Pevsner and E. Hubbard, *The Buildings of England: Cheshire,* Penguin, 1971

Waterways World Guides: Trent and Mersey Canal (North), Shropshire Union Canal , Llangollen Canal

walkers who enjoy the challenge of the hills, and adds the extra element of exploring the narrow-gauge and light railways of yesteryear. A large area is covered, stretching from Burnley in the north, to Stoke-on-Trent in the south. A total of 18 walks is included, each accompanied by a detailed sketch map, many photographs of the old railways in action.

ISBN: 1 85058 215 7 £5.95

West Pennine Walks - Mike Cresswell; photographs by Reg Timms

Personal anecdotes, maps and detailed directions enhance these 32 walks between 5 and 20 miles that are easily accessible. They are all based in this beautiful and varied area which, although popular with the 'locals', remains undiscovered by many. Mike entertains with humour, zest and enthusiasm.

ISBN:1 85058 093 6 £5.95

Staffordshire Walks: Simply Superb - Les Lumsdon

Containing nearly 30 walks, this offers both gentle strolls through Staffordshire's pleasant countryside and some of the best hill walking for miles around. Walk through villages, along canal towpaths and in peaceful woods of this undiscovered haven for walkers. Endless ideas for enjoyable days out and places to visit.

ISBN: 1 85058 105 3 £4.95

Shropshire Walks - Les Lumsdon

The 36 walks are located in all parts of Shropshire. Several feature fine hill walking on the Welsh borderlands, including stretches along Offa's Dyke, The Long Mynd and Caer Caradoc. Others start from delightful villages and hamlets in the North and East of the County, such as Acton Burnell, Myddle, Stottesdon and Welshampton. Many of the walks are 5-6 miles in length to suit the interested walker looking for a pleasant day out. A few are shorter to meet family requirements and an equal number feature longer more demanding walks for those who like to set a pace.

ISBN: 1 85058 160 6 £4.95

Great Walks from Welsh Railways - Les Lumsdon and Colin Speakman

Two of the best-known names to enthusiasts of trains and walking, Les and Colin explore Wales with the help of the 'great little trains' as well as the usual BR locomotion. It features many of BR's most scenic lines, the fascination of narrow gauge steam and presents the walks against a backdrop of scenic splendour and cultural heritage. Twenty walks are included, together with detailed maps and directions. Endorsed by PrysEdwards, Chairman of the Wales Tourist Board.

ISBN:1 85058 104 5 £4.95

Twenty Great Walks from British Rail - Les Lumsdon and Colin Speakman

This volume covers selected areas in the UK, with at least one local walk for every holiday visitor and the opportunity to cover the entire country by rail and foot. Detailed sketch maps and directions are included. *ISBN: 1 85058 099 7 £4.95*

Town Guides and Local History

Portrait of Warrington - Jen Darling

Jen Darling, in her second book for Sigma, turns her attention to her home town of Warrington. It is packed with information from the early Roman settlementto the economic expansion of the New Town. The special character of this book is the emphasis on Warrington's people - how they live and how they've coped with the fast pace of change in their area.
ISBN: 1 85058 207 6 £4.95

Portrait of: Macclesfield - Doug Pickford

The author is the editor of a local newspaper and has a unique collection of photographs of the Macclesfield area. Many will know his regular column and 'picture and a song' shows. Old Macclesfield and its picturesque surrounding villages are presented alongside present-day photographs. A town trail is included to enhance the enjoyment of this excellent book.
ISBN: 1 85058 113 4 £4.95

Portrait of: Wilmslow, Handforth and Alderley Edge - Ron Lee

Using the same approach as the Macclesfield book, old and new Wilmslow are presented so that the reader can see how things have changed. As an added bonus, it includes town trails for Handforth, Wilmslow and Alderley Edge. Many unusual stories about the area are retold with great style by journalist, Ron Lee.
ISBN: 1 85058 120 7 £4.95

Portrait of: Knutsford - Geoffrey King

This delightful and picturesque old Cheshire town owes much to Mrs Gaskell's 'Cranford' and the unique architecture of R H Watt; but Knutsford is now rapidly developing both as a commuter town, and as a major tourist centre with one of England's premier National Trust attractions, Tatton Park. Geoffrey King is a travel lecturer whose pen and camera paint a captivating portrait of this outstanding part of Cheshire.
ISBN: 1 85058 122 3 £4.95

Portrait of: Manchester - John Creighton

This is a further member of our series, but with a slightly different emphasis. Although it also combines both old and new photo-

graphs, it presents them in groups relating to such themes as: the architectural heritage, transport, recreation, commerce and education. A perfect souvenir and an ideal introduction to this city.
ISBN: 1 85058 121 5 £4.95

Portrait of: Stockport - John Creighton
The town's history is presented in a readable form, and this is followed with sections to illustrate aspects of Stockport today. Even the casual visitor, whose first view of Stockport may be above or below its railway viaduct of 27 arches and 11 million bricks. And that's just one of the surprises in this book.
ISBN: 1 85058 135 5 £4.95

Portrait of: Buxton and District - John Creighton
Until now, there has been no popular history of Buxton, but this book relates the history of the town, its local industry and commerce. Customs and traditions such as well dressing and rush bearing are illustrated, together with the many places of interest - including Castleton, Chatsworth and Haddon - all within 30 minutes drive from Buxton.
ISBN: 1 85058 161 4 £4.95

The History of Sale - Norman V. Swain
This is the first comprehensive history of Sale. It is packed from cover to cover with fascinating facts and photographs of immense interest to those who know this pleasant town and to all those who want to know how and why modern towns have evolved from primitive beginnings. Norman Swain – an active member of the Lancashire and Cheshire Antiquarian Society - wrote this book to appeal to local people, schoolchildren and researchers.
ISBN: 1 85058 086 3 £4.95

Cheshire: a portrait in words and pictures - John Creighton
Whatever your interests - history, places to visit, old churches or even public houses - you'll derive many hours of pleasure from this book. Chester is covered in great detail, with the county's thriving agricultural community, industry, transport and communications. An ideal souvenir of the area.
ISBN: 1-85058-092-8 £4.95

SIGMA LEISURE is an imprint of SIGMA PRESS. Order all Sigma books from your usual bookseller, or contact: Sigma Press, 1 South Oak Lane, Wilmslow, Cheshire SK9 6AR.

Phone: 0625-531035. Fax: 0625-536800